Natural Parasite Management for Livestock

Harnessing Nature's Solutions for Internal Control and Healthy Herds

Table of Contents

Introduction

As a livestock owner, you're probably no stranger to the daily rituals of tending to your animals, ensuring they're well-fed, comfortable, and healthy. But have you ever noticed those subtle signs that something might not be quite right? Perhaps your chickens' combs have lost their vibrant red hue, or you've noticed a horse or cow looking a bit more "ribby" than usual. Even your sheep's once rosy eyelids now appear paler than they should be. It's easy to dismiss these small changes as part of the natural ebb and flow of livestock care, but these indicators may be telling you something crucial – your animals might be under attack from parasites.

Parasites can be silent predators, slowly sapping the vitality and well-being of your livestock. They lurk beneath the surface, affecting your animals in ways that may not be immediately evident. The reality is that managing parasites can become a relentless, full-time job, especially if you're committed to doing it without resorting to chemical solutions. But what if there was a way to shift this burden from an all-consuming endeavor to a part-time, seasonal one that you and your livestock could benefit from?

A pale comb and wattles may be the first indication of a possible parasite problem for chickens. Rest assured, though, by developing a systematic approach, you can transform the daunting task of parasite control into a manageable and sustainable practice. This transformation is achievable through several key strategies:

- **Pasture Management and Rotation**: You must learn to optimize your pasture management techniques and rotation practices to minimize the risk of parasitic infestations. Careful management of grazing areas can reduce exposure to parasites, giving your livestock more than a fighting chance to flourish.
- **Environmental Control**: Learn to implement effective measures to create an environment less conducive to parasites. By making your livestock's living conditions less hospitable for these intruders, you can reduce the prevalence of parasitic infections.
- **Targeted Deworming with Natural Products**: Embrace the power of natural solutions for deworming, possibly even growing some of the preventative ingredients yourself. Discover how to use targeted deworming strategies with organic and sustainable products, ensuring that you only treat when necessary, minimizing the risk of resistance.
- **Continual Research and Learning**: Stay up-to-date with the latest developments in parasite control for livestock. An ongoing commitment to research and education is essential in adapting to new challenges and optimizing your parasite management strategies.

A healthy and vibrant livestock operation is within your reach. Healthy chickens should have bright combs, shiny feathers, and lively spirits, while cows, horses, and sheep should showcase the robustness that's the hallmark of well-cared-for animals. While specific symptoms are associated with particular parasites, it's crucial to remember that these indicators are not definitive diagnoses. High parasitic loads can lead to various issues, including diarrhea, dehydration, weight loss, and lethargy, regardless of the specific parasite responsible. But don't worry; this book is here to guide you.

As you start this journey to reclaim the health of your livestock, remember that you're not alone. There is a world of resources out there, starting with this comprehensive book! So, dive right into the world of sustainable and holistic livestock care.

Chapter 1: What Are Livestock Parasites?

To give you a foundation for the information you'll learn from the book, this chapter explores various types of parasites that affect livestock, their groups, background, life cycles, and their potential impact on animal health and productivity. It also emphasizes the importance of understanding and managing these parasites in livestock production.

History and Background of Livestock Parasites

Parasites are living beings living inside or on the surface of another organism (known as a host), taking nutrients from the latter. Livestock and other animals can be affected by over 1000 parasite species, some of which can also be transmitted to humans.

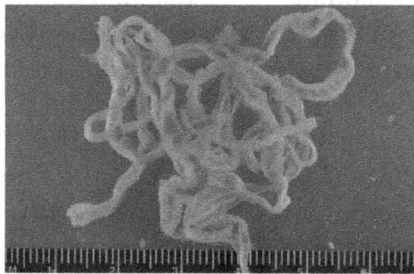

Parasites are living beings living inside or on the surface of another organism (known as a host), taking nutrients from the latter.

FWC Fish and Wildlife Research Institute, CC BY-NC-ND 2.0 DEED

Parasites, in a veterinary study field called parasitology, have their roots in ancient civilizations. Ancient Egyptian records suggest that Egyptians studied parasites and described larger ectoparasites (or external parasites) in humans but didn't understand the organism's life cycle. Similar parasites are believed to have affected the Israelites during their voyages; they described them as fiery serpents. The first to recognize that parasites had several stages during their life cycle was Aristotle, who noted cysts of worms in pigs' tongues. Scientists also theorize that the Hebrews prohibited pig consumption because they likely discovered similar cysts in these animals.

From the first century onward, interest in parasites grew intensely. At the beginning of the second century CE, Aretaeus noted finding several fluid-filled bladders in animals, and a century later, Galen described three distinct types of parasites in humans. In the 7th century, Paulus Aegineta studied human helminths even more, naming one of the groups Ascarides. These small worms, located in the lower intestines of people and warm-blooded animals, are the group of tapeworms and ascarid worms now known as Ascaris.

A Byzantine physician named Alexander authored the first book about parasitic worms, *De Lombrices* (translated as "on worms"), establishing the foundation of modern parasitology. However, at this time, scientists and scholars only knew that parasites cause diseases, but not how they came to the host and how to prevent this. The source of parasitic infection was identified at the beginning of the 11th century when Ibn Zuhr (an Islamic Moroccan physician) and Abbess Hildegard of Bingen (an animal health writer and researcher) both concluded that mites transmitted scabies.

Parasitology understanding was expanded during the Middle Ages when Albertus Magnus wrote about parasitic worms (helminths in contemporary literature) in fish, horses, falcons, and dogs in his book *De Animalibus* in 1478. A couple of decades later, Anthony Fitzherbert described the disease that was caused by the liver fluke in his work *A Newe Treate or Treatise Most Profytable for All Husbandmen*. He even concluded that the source of the infection was wet, marshy land where snails also lived, but he didn't understand the parasites' life cycle enough to make a connection between the snails and the infected animals. In his first classification of animals, Linnaeus wrote about fasciola hepatica, described as a leech whose young thrive in water. Because the parasitic cycle was not understood until much later, people believed that parasites are spontaneously generated in the bodies of people and animals.

William Harvey's discovery of the heart's role in blood circulation was one of the earliest discoveries that cast doubt on the hypothesis of spontaneous genesis. In addition to describing this theory in his dissertation On Animal Generation (published in 1651), Harvey contends that all living things originate from eggs instead of spontaneously emerging. Dutch biologist Jan Swammerdam described several life forms of insects, including adult, pupa, larva, and egg, proving that these animals go through an entire cycle during their lifetime, proving that they didn't come from nowhere.

In the 17th century, Italian physician Francesco Redi noted, removed, and examined ticks and lice from people and animals. Redi described the "louse" as one of the diseases these parasites caused, for which he became known as the "father of parasitology." Through a simple experiment, he also once and for all proved the theory of accidental generation invalid. Laying two cuts of meat on a plate, he covered one, leaving the other one uncovered. The latter soon attracted flies, which laid eggs on it, and in two days, the meat was infested with maggots.

In contrast, the covered piece of meat did not have any maggots in it. Confirming Redi's findings, Dutch microscopist Antonie van Leeuwenhoek observed protozoan parasites under the microscope and sketched them. These were parasites found in peoples' and animals' intestines, often causing diarrhea. English physician Edward Tyson studied and examined the nematode Ascaris lumbricoides, ultimately finding that the parasite had two sexes (which alludes to sexual reproduction) and further disproving the theory of random generation in parasitic worms.

Numerous animal and human parasites were found and characterized during the 17th and 18th centuries. Johann Goeze documented the ascaris worms in pigs, while Peter Simon Pallas reported the hydatid cysts in people and the cat tapeworm (taenia crassiceps) in 1766. Swedish and German botanists published three tomes systemizing parasite species in 1819, establishing a standard reference that was considered valid until the parasite life cycle was fully understood. In 1863, German physician and pathologist Rudolph Virchow suggested that a more vigorous pig meat infection could prevent trichinosis infection in people.

After discovering a previously unidentified worm in the bile duct of a giraffe, British doctor TC Cobbold set out to study and perfect the current parasitic systemization. In 1878, he presented the discovery of a filaria embryo in a mosquito's body, which led to the concept that ties mosquitos to the disease known as malaria. Two years later, Griffith Evans discovered that the first pathogenic trypanosome, Trypanosoma evansi, was the cause of a tropical illness that affected horses and camels.

With these and similar discoveries in the mid to late 19th century, parasitology became a well-established field of study in veterinary medicine. Scientists also began to look into the parasite life cycles even more, which allowed them to come up with effective control, prevention, and treatment measures for the diseases they caused. People recognized that some parasites, like trichinella and other worms, represented severe public health hazards and had a great need to control their spread. By investigating these and other parasites affecting livestock, control measures for liver fluke, lungworms, trypanosomiasis, coccidia, haemonchosis, roundworms, and other parasites were developed and successfully implemented.

Why Is Parasite Control Important in Animal Husbandry?

Both external and internal parasites can cause health issues in animals, weakening their immune system and predisposing them to bacterial and other infections. They might also cause damage on their own depending on how they feed on the host and whether they carry and transmit other diseases. Infected livestock can also transmit the parasites or the secondary diseases they carry to humans and other animals. All these led to significant economic losses, just as they did since people started domesticating animals and rearing them for food and other purposes. For all these reasons, controlling parasitic proliferation in animal husbandry is of utmost importance. Fortunately, due to all the discoveries of parasitology nowadays, there are numerous measures for control and prevention.

Common Livestock Parasites

Livestock parasites are divided into two major categories – internal and external. The internal ones enter the animal's body, feed on it, and damage it from the inside, while the external ones attack and infect from the outside. Based on whether they are transmitted to animals from another source, parasites can also be vector or non-vector-borne. Vector-borne organisms are typically internal as well.

Internal Parasites and Diseases
Coccidia

Coccidiosis is caused by the protozoan Eimeria sp., commonly known as coccidia. They live in farm animals' intestinal walls and are host-specific. In other words, the variant that infects cattle will not infect goats and sheep. While coccidia is normally present in animals, over-proliferation can cause infestation and diseases. The latter typically happens in young specimens lacking sufficient immunity (premature weaning, cold climate, etc.) to prevent proliferation or in older animals in overcrowded or stressful conditions. Coccidia is transmitted by feces, which can remain infectious on the ground for up to six days and spreads very quickly in warm and wet conditions.

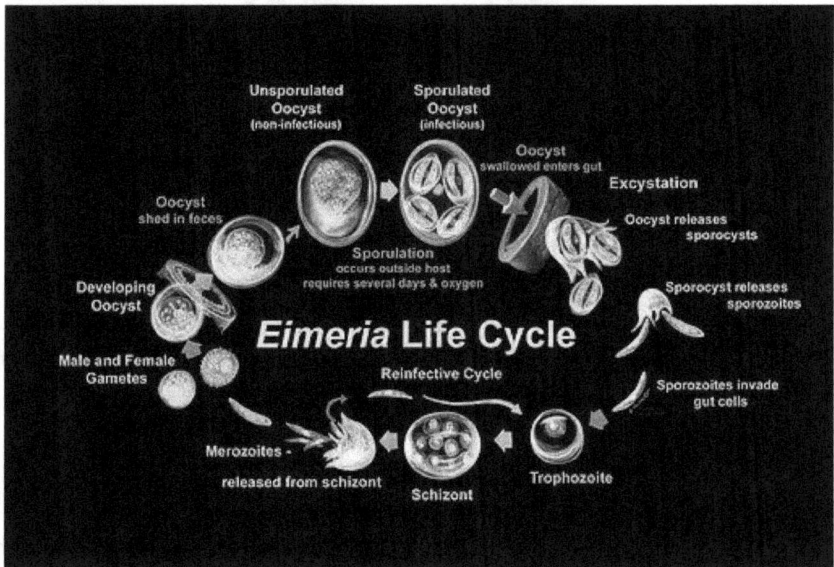

While coccidia is normally present in animals, over-proliferation can cause infestation and diseases.
https://commons.wikimedia.org/wiki/File:Eimeria_life_cycle_usda.jpg

Nematodes – Gastrointestinal Worms

Most worms in the gastrointestinal (GIT) tract of livestock are nematodes. While this specific group of worms has several common features, not all prefer the same conditions (for example, some prefer warmer climates, while others thrive in cold weather). Young animals are at a higher risk, but GIT worms can affect other specimens, too, if those have lower immunity to intestinal parasites (like bulls, for example).

Expelled from the GIT tract, parasitic nematodes can survive on the ground for several days – the exact length depends on the climate conditions and whether they have a nutrient source available.

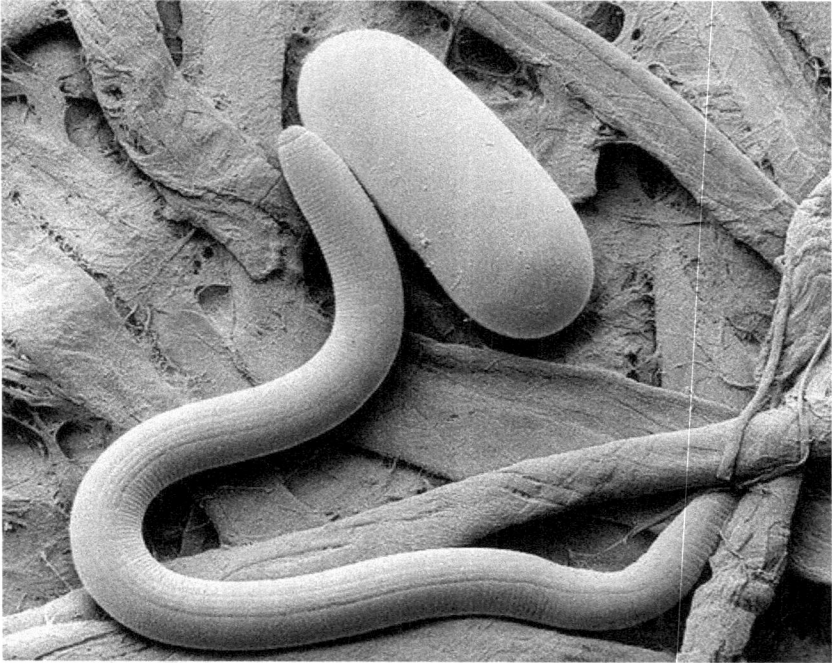

Expelled from the GIT tract, parasitic nematodes can survive on the ground for several days.
https://commons.wikimedia.org/wiki/File:Soybean_cyst_nematode_and_egg_SEM.jpg

Liver Fluke

Caused by the parasitic trematodes platyhelminths, liver fluke is a zoonotic disease that, while common in livestock, can also infect other animals and people. The worms live in the liver and bile ducts and can't survive on the ground for more than two days. However, they have another host, snails, making areas like marshes, springs, coastal regions, irrigated pastures, water troughs, etc., potential sources of infection.

Theileriosis

Theileriosis is a vector-borne disease transmitted by ticks and, on rare occasions, by other biting animals or reused veterinary injection needles. It's brought on by theileria orientalis, a blood parasite causing anemia. The parasite can survive on surface food for 12-24 hours, depending on conditions.

Trichomoniasis

Caused by the protozoan parasite tritrichomonas foetus, trichomoniasis is a venereal disease that lives in the host's genital tract, often leading to loss of embryo, abortion, and stillbirth in female animals. It is transmitted via mating or insemination, but the parasite can survive on non-live surfaces for up to 24 hours.

Toxoplasmosis

Caused by the protozoan parasite Toxoplasma gondii, toxoplasmosis is another zoonotic disease disseminated by infected feces or, in some cases, by rodent bites. It can also be transmitted by animals eating infected tissue of other animals. The parasite lives for several days in a cyst or asexual reproductive form in the dung and other surfaces.

External Parasites and Diseases

Flies are common livestock parasites, and depending on the species, they can cause issues on their own or transmit vector-borne diseases. For example, buffalo flies bite and feed on the animal's blood by latching onto its skin and laying eggs on its dung. They can travel over six miles in search of a host. Animals in poor condition and those with darker coatings are more likely to attract flies. The same animals are more at risk of contracting flystrike, caused by blowflies laying their eggs on the animals (in wounds, unclean mucous surfaces like nose, genitalia, etc.). Flystrike is an extremely painful and often fatal condition. Nuisance flies, on the other hand, only feed and breed in the dung – however, for the same reason, they carry diseases, which, when transmitted from feces, can infect livestock.

Ticks

While ticks often have specific hosts (for example, cattle ticks will only feed on and infect cattle), they can also survive on other animals and humans. Female ticks drop off their eggs on the same animal they feed on. The larvae hatch, develop in nymphs, and become adults within 21 days, often remaining attached and feeding on the same animal. Ticks are carriers of vector-borne diseases, and some species will cause health issues on their own.

Tick Fever

Caused by blood parasites and transmitted by ticks, tick fever is a serious disease that destroys the host's blood cells, affecting several organs and often leading to death.

Tick Paralysis

Ixodes holocyclus is a tick species that secrete a toxin in its saliva, which causes paralysis in animals and people. Small farm animals are more vulnerable than larger livestock due to the amount of toxin per body mass ratio. This is a three-host tick. Each phase has its host, but only adults can cause paralysis. The larvae and nymph stages are vulnerable and can survive only a few hours without a host. The same applies to bush ticks, which transmit the blood parasite Theileria orientalis to warm-blooded animals.

Lice

Livestock is vulnerable to both sucking and biting lice, both host-specific external parasites. Biting lice feeds (bovicola sp.) latch onto the nasal skin and feed on the skin and the bacteria that grows there. Sucking lice (linognathus sp.), on the other hand, have a specific mouthpiece that can penetrate the animal's skin, enabling them to feed on its blood.

Livestock Parasites Life Cycles and Control Measures

Here are the life cycles of common livestock parasites and the stages where control measures should be implemented.

Nematodes

With a few exceptions, most nematodes have a similar life cycle, which is as follows:

1. The adult female nematodes lay their eggs in the animal's GIT.

2. The eggs are expelled into the dung.

3. While in the dung, the eggs develop into first-stage larvae, then molt to second-stage larvae (since they are less mobile, the larvae are more vulnerable to antiparasitic measures).

4. Feeding on the animals' dung, the larvae reach the second molt stage and develop into third-stage larvae.

5. The third-stage larvae are more mobile and migrate to the vegetation where the animals graze and ingest them (before ingestion, the infection can still be controlled by preventative grazing measures).

6. Once ingested, the third-stage larvae develop into fourth-stage larvae in two to five days.

7. After 14 days, the fourth-stage larvae become adult nematodes that can live up to several months, feeding and reproducing.

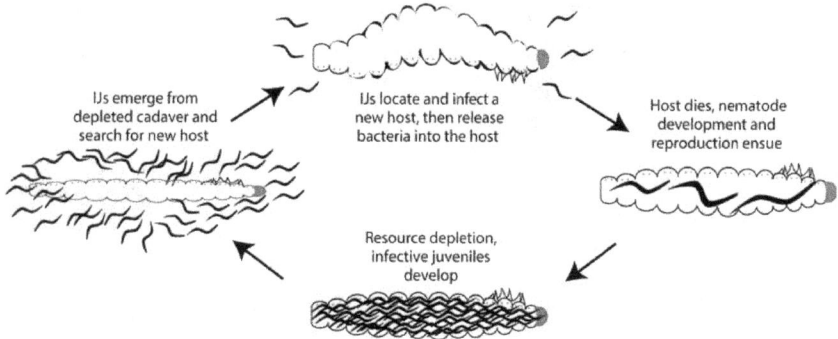

IJs emerge from depleted cadaver and search for new host

IJs locate and infect a new host, then release bacteria into the host

Host dies, nematode development and reproduction ensue

Resource depletion, infective juveniles develop

With a few exceptions, most nematodes have a similar life cycle.
Adler Dillman, CC BY 4.0 <https://creativecommons.org/licenses/by/4.0>, via Wikimedia Commons: https://commons.wikimedia.org/wiki/File:EPN_Lifecycle.tif

Toxoplasma

Toxoplasma has livestock as its definitive host for both asexual and sexual reproduction. Depending on the stage upon ingestion, the toxoplasma life cycle can last between a few days (for bradyzoites) and three weeks (for tachyzoites). The full lifecycle is as follows:

1. After the process of sexual reproduction, the parasites produce oocysts, which are expelled from the animal body through feces a few weeks after the infection – this is the time when control measures are the most effective as they can prevent the rest of the cycle.

2. The oocysts contain sporocysts, and within a few days, four sporozoites develop within the sporocysts, beginning the sporulation process (asexual reproduction) –the fastest phase of reproduction.

3. When another animal ingests the sporulated oocysts (bradyzoites), the sporozoites exit the oocyst and invade the animal's small intestine, where they enter the enterocytes (intestinal cells) – the pace of reproduction slows down.

4. Alternatively, the sporozoites can invade the host's blood and lymph cells (by going through the intestinal wall) and become tachyzoites.

11

5. As tachyzoites, they reach the tissues, where they develop into bradyzoites contained in tissue cysts in cardiac and skeletal muscle, eyes, and nervous system tissues – control and antiparasitic measures can be implemented here to kill the cysts and boost the animal's immunity to prevent cyst development.

6. Tachyzoites can also be expelled if they reach the intestines (and consequently be ingested by other animals).

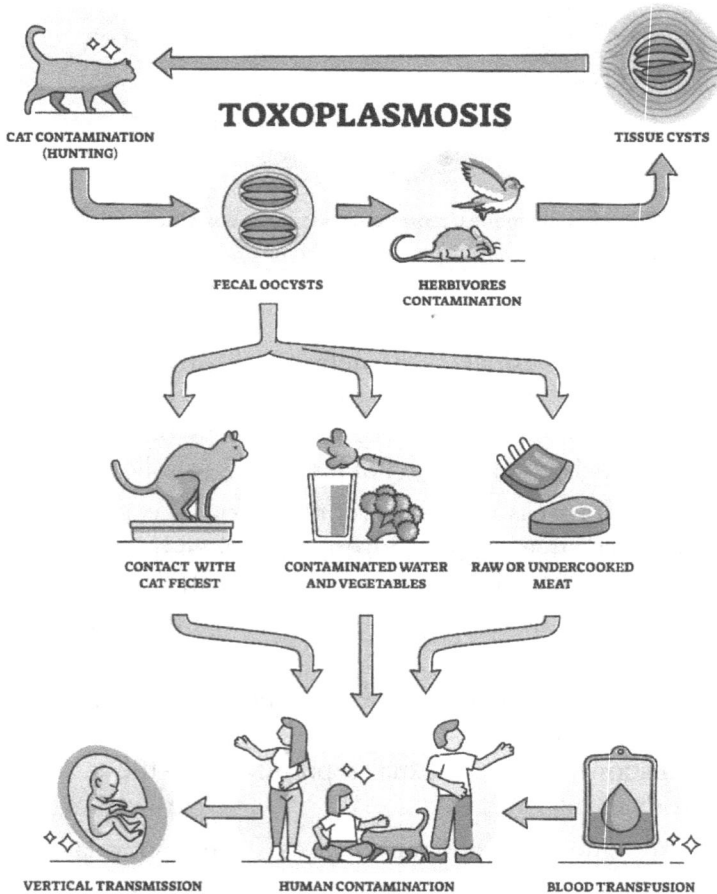

TOXOPLASMOSIS

CAT CONTAMINATION (HUNTING)

TISSUE CYSTS

FECAL OOCYSTS

HERBIVORES CONTAMINATION

CONTACT WITH CAT FECEST

CONTAMINATED WATER AND VEGETABLES

RAW OR UNDERCOOKED MEAT

VERTICAL TRANSMISSION

HUMAN CONTAMINATION

BLOOD TRANSFUSION

Toxoplasma has livestock as its definitive host for both asexual and sexual reproduction.

Liver Fluke

As a two-host parasite, liver fluke has snails and livestock as its first and definitive hosts. The full cycle is as follows:

1. The parasite produces eggs in the snail, where they develop into first-stage larvae – without the interaction of the host, the cycle can't be completed, so preventing it is a crucial control and antiparasitic measure.

2. The first phase larvae exit the snails and get to the herbage, forming cysts.

3. The grazing animals consume the cysts, which break, and the larvae continue to develop.

4. The larvae get through their intestinal wall and into the liver, where they become adults feeding on the bile duct.

5. Through the bile, the adult worms get into the feces, producing eggs expelled into the dung.

6. The eggs are consumed by snails, where the cycle continues (the entire cycle lasts up to 21 days.

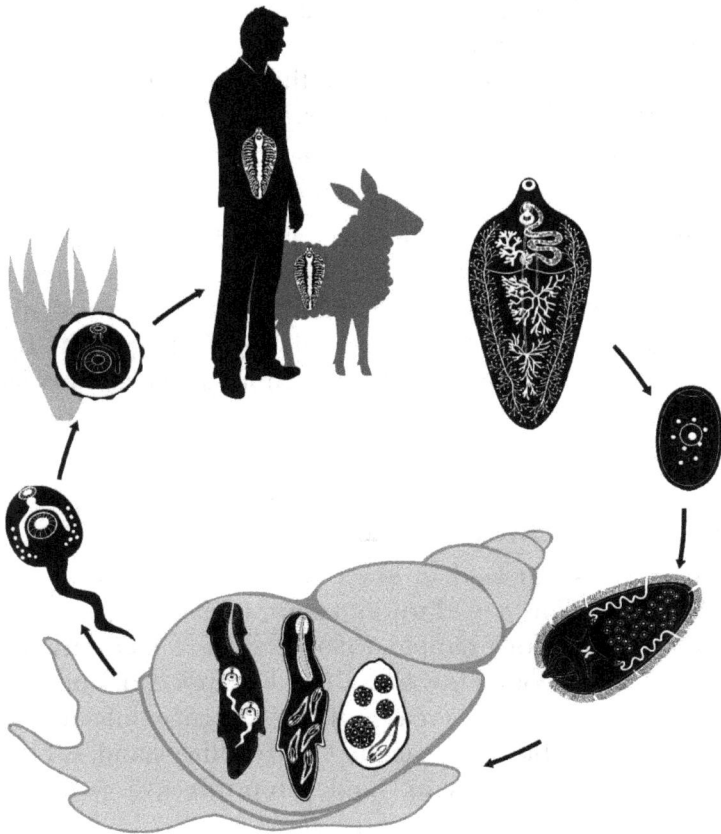

As a two-host parasite, liver fluke has snails and livestock as its first and definitive hosts.

The Negative Effects of Parasitic Infections

Livestock parasites have numerous adverse effects which impact animal welfare and cause economic losses for farmers. Below are the negative effects of parasitic infections in livestock.

Impaired Liveweight Gain

Feeding in the host's intestines, GIT parasites divert nutrients from the host, which results in its inability to gain weight. However, external parasites and vector-borne diseases can also have the same effect as they cause circulatory and gastrointestinal issues and reduced appetite. Depending on the type of animals in question and the degree of parasitic infection, weight gain can be reduced by up to 90 pounds.

Effect on Milk Production

Certain parasites affecting the internal organs could also cause reduced milk production in lactating animals. This is a particularly economically devastating effect for animals raised for their milk. Younger female specimens (those in their first or second lactation period) are more affected by intensive parasitic infections and are more at risk of having reduced milk production.

Reduced Meat Quality

Since many livestock animals are raised for their meat, parasite infection reducing carcass quality can also represent a significant issue. Nematodes are particularly problematic as they form cysts in the muscles, reducing their quality and hindering their growth. Instead of muscle, some of these animals will grow more subcutaneous fat, which isn't as profitable. Other parasites that cause reduced appetite, GIT issues, and limited blood and nutrient distribution through the body can have similar effects.

Impaired Reproductive Performance

Certain parasites can lead to lowered conception rate and breeding ability in livestock. This is tied to the failure to gain weight and the type of parasitic infection. For example, toxoplasmosis is a commonly known cause of infertility in young livestock. The likelihood of conception and regular breeding intervals increases if the parasitic infection is cured before animals reach breeding weight. On the other hand, GIT parasites rarely cause infertility issues or hinder reproductive performance in livestock.

Increased Mortality Rate

Parasitic infection can increase livestock mortality rates for two reasons. If the parasites cause symptoms that lead to the animal's failure to flourish and inability to heal, they can lead to the animal's death. For example, certain GIT worms can lead to a 100% mortality rate in animals aged one to three months. The young specimens have a smaller intestinal tract, which the worms obstruct, preventing the animal from taking in any nutrients. In adult livestock, this rarely happens because their GIT track is larger. Besides the immediate cause, parasites can also be an indirect cause of livestock mortality because they compromise the immune system, so the animals succumb to other, far more serious conditions. For instance, if a worm larva or cyst migrates to the lungs, this can cause pneumonia or toxemia, resulting from the organism's inability to fight off infections.

Effects on Public Health

Certain parasitic infections (like Trichinos or tapeworms) can harm public health. These parasites can infect humans and other animals if inadequate control measures aren't implemented. Treating these secondary infections further strains the economic burden of parasite management.

How Seasonal Variations Affect the Prevalence of Parasitic Infections

Seasonal variations in weather and climate can influence the prevalence and intensity of parasitic infections. For example, most protozoans show a greater presence in the warmer months (May to September). By contrast, nematodes are more likely to cause infections in winter (December to February). This is likely because free livestock breeding is more frequent from spring through autumn, which creates ideal conditions for protozoan infections. While grazing in open pastures, livestock is more exposed to external parasites and can also ingest internal ones. During the winter months, the animals are often kept in a closed space, and their nutrition is controlled (they have lower chances of ingesting parasites), which lowers the prevalence of some parasitic infections. Moreover, protozoans are more affected by seasonal changes and changes in temperature on a day-to-day basis, while nematodes aren't.

If the animals are kept in a closed space during the winter and gather around a small feeding area, this further increases the chances of parasitic infections caused by nematodes. During the warmer months (and in warm, enclosed spaces), nematode larvae can move quickly and will consume more nutrients. When nutrients are scarce, the larvae will stop moving to conserve energy. If they can't find more nutrients, they'll die. The increased water loss during the summer further accelerates this process. In colder climates and seasons, the larvae won't move as quickly because they require more energy to do that. They can, however, curl up and form a protective cyst, which allows them to survive for up to several months, depending on the species and climate conditions.

Some worms, like the brown stomach worm or the black scour worm, prefer wet and cold conditions, especially in moderate climates, where the winters are characterized by higher temperatures and heavy rainfalls. Other worms, such as the barber's pole worm, for example, prefer warm conditions and regions with heavy rainfall or increased irrigation. If livestock graze pastures with large amounts of precipitation (natural or artificial) during the summer, they'll be more likely exposed to this worm.

Fly larvae prefer warm conditions, so the prevalence of flies and fly strikes is higher during the warmer months than during the winter. The risk of flystrike increases during the spring as soon as temperatures reach above 63 degrees Fahrenheit. Rainfalls and moderate wind conditions in spring through autumn further increase the prevalence of flies and fly larva development in manure, natural vegetation, and other places where flies are attracted (for example, where urine accumulates).

Interestingly enough, lice have no preference for climate conditions and can proliferate just as easily during the winter as they do during the warmer months. Like flies, lice eggs and larvae will survive in vegetation and on the surfaces and animals in an enclosed space. Sucking lice are more likely to cause a parasitic infestation during the winter when the animals are kept inside.

Chapter 2: Clinical Signs and Diagnosis

Parasitic infections in livestock can have devastating economic and health implications for farmers and ranchers. These outbreaks and infections lead to reduced productivity, weight loss, and, in severe cases, mortality. To manage this situation effectively, it is essential to recognize and diagnose these conditions accurately. This chapter explores common parasitic infections in each livestock species, focusing on identifying and diagnosing them effectively.

Parasites and Livestock

Whether it's a small farm with a few animals or an industrial-scale livestock farming operation, these infections, when left unattended, result in many challenges, including economic losses, animal suffering, and environmental consequences. To develop a clear perspective, here's why timely recognition and diagnosis of parasitic infections in livestock is necessary.

Animal Welfare

On-time recognition and diagnosis of parasite infection or outbreak is crucial to establish animal health and welfare. The discomfort, pain, and suffering livestock animals experience can be alleviated through early intervention. These parasitic infections, if left unattended, can even result in severe conditions that lead to organ damage and, in some cases, even death.

Economic Impact

No matter the number of animals you care for, it's necessary for livestock farming to be economically sustainable. Parasitic infections and diseases will decrease productivity as animals face issues like weight loss, reduced milk or egg production, and lowered reproductive performance. All these factors can have a severe economic impact if not handled properly.

Prevention of Parasite Spread

When you diagnose parasitic infections early, you'll be in a good position to prevent them from spreading by quarantining infected animals quickly. This proactive approach helps to protect the rest of the population from potential outbreaks and minimizes the need for extensive treatments.

Targeted Treatment

Accurate diagnosis enables veterinarians and livestock owners to develop customized treatment strategies. This tailored approach reduces the unnecessary use of medication and minimizes the risk of drug resistance. By focusing on treating only infected animals, farmers can achieve cost savings.

Environmental Impact

Recognizing and diagnosing parasitic infections also has positive environmental implications. Treating infected animals minimizes the spread of parasites through their feces, which benefits the local ecosystem and other livestock sharing the same environment.

Food Safety

Parasitic infections in livestock can affect the safety and quality of meat, milk, and eggs. Through accurate diagnosis and subsequent treatment, livestock owners can ensure that these products meet safety and quality standards, safeguarding the health of consumers and preserving the reputation of farming operations.

Research and Epidemiology

Accurate diagnosis of parasitic infections offers valuable data for research and epidemiological studies. This information aids scientists in understanding the prevalence and distribution of parasitic infections in different livestock populations. Such research forms the basis for developing more effective control and prevention strategies, ultimately benefiting the livestock industry.

In various regions, legal requirements exist for controlling and treating infections in livestock. Proper diagnosis and adherence to these regulations are essential to prevent potential legal consequences, ensuring compliance with local laws and regulations.

Common Clinical Signs

Clinical signs of various animal health conditions can be categorized based on the affected organ systems or body parts. Here are some common clinical signs you can find in different organ systems.

Gastrointestinal Signs:

- **Diarrhea**: Common in gastrointestinal parasitic infections, diarrhea can vary in severity and may contain mucus or blood.

- **Weight Loss:** Parasites can lead to chronic weight loss due to reduced nutrient absorption.

- **Decreased Appetite:** Infected animals may eat less, resulting in malnutrition.

- **Bottle Jaw (Edema of the Lower Jaw):** Swelling under the jaw due to edema and anemia, often seen in small ruminants with heavy gastrointestinal worm burdens.

- **Dehydration:** Persistent diarrhea can cause dehydration, sunken eyes, dry mucous membranes, and decreased skin elasticity.

- **Abdominal Pain:** Some animals may exhibit colic or discomfort in response to gastrointestinal parasites.

- **Submandibular Edema (Brisket Disease):** Swelling under the jaw or in the brisket area, common in cattle with high parasite loads.

Dermatological Signs:

- **Hair Loss (Alopecia):** Parasitic skin infections, such as mange mites, can lead to hair loss and skin irritation.

Parasitic skin infections, such as mange mites, can lead to hair loss and skin irritation.
Alan R Walker, CC BY-SA 3.0 <https://creativecommons.org/licenses/by-sa/3.0>, via Wikimedia Commons: https://commons.wikimedia.org/wiki/File:Sweating-sickness-Zimbabwe.jpg

- **Skin Lesions:** Skin conditions like dermatophytosis result in scabs and crusts on the skin.
- **Intense Scratching or Rubbing:** Animals may scratch or rub excessively due to itching caused by parasites, leading to hair loss and skin damage.
- **Pruritus:** Intense itching is a symptom of various skin parasites, causing animals to scratch and rub their skin raw.
- **Crusting and Scaling:** Affected areas may develop crusts, scales, or flakiness due to skin irritation.

Respiratory Signs:

- **Coughing:** Lungworm infections can lead to coughing and respiratory distress, particularly in cattle and small ruminants.
- **Nasal Discharge:** Seen in cases of lungworm and nasal bot infections, with mucus or nasal discharge from the nostrils.
- **Dyspnea:** Respiratory distress and difficult breathing can occur in severe cases of lungworm infection.
- **Crackles and Wheezes:** Abnormal lung sounds may be auscultated in animals with lungworm infections.

Ocular Signs:

- **Conjunctivitis:** In cattle and sheep, eye irritation and inflammation occur with certain eye-dwelling parasites, such as thelazia.

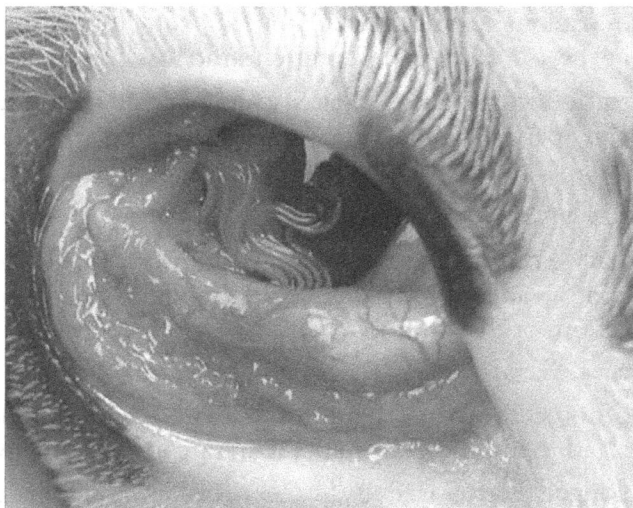

In cattle and sheep, eye irritation and inflammation occur with certain eye-dwelling parasites, such as thelazia.

https://commons.wikimedia.org/wiki/File:Thelazia_callipaeda_in_dog.jpg

- **Ocular Discharge:** Excessive tearing or discharge from the eyes may result from irritation by eye parasites or migration of larvae in the eyes.

- **Corneal Opacities:** Clouding or opacities in the cornea can be seen in cases of parasitic keratitis.

- **Corneal Ulcers:** Ulcerations on the cornea may result from parasitic eye infections, causing pain and discomfort.

Neurological Signs:

- **Circling or Head Tilt:** Signs of neural larval migrans caused by certain parasites, such as Baylisascaris, leading to incoordination and abnormal head movements.

- **Incoordination or Paralysis:** Infestations with certain parasites can affect the nervous system, causing incoordination and paralysis in affected animals.

- **Tremors or Seizures:** Some parasitic infections can lead to tremors or seizures, affecting muscle coordination.

Hematological Signs:

- **Anemia:** Blood-feeding parasites like ticks and haemonchus worms can lead to anemia, resulting in pale mucous membranes and weakness.
- **Pale Mucous Membranes:** Anemia, characterized by pale gums and eyes, is a common sign due to the loss of red blood cells.
- **Thrombocytopenia:** A decrease in platelet count results from certain parasitic infections, increasing the risk of bleeding disorders.

Urogenital Signs:

- **Urinary Tract Infections:** Certain parasites can affect the urinary system, leading to signs like frequent urination, painful urination, or discomfort.

Reproductive Signs:

- **Abortions:** Protozoal parasites like neospora and toxoplasma can lead to abortions in cattle, resulting in reproductive losses.
- **Prolonged Estrus (Heat):** Some parasitic infections can disrupt the estrous cycle, leading to prolonged or irregular periods of heat.
- **Reduced Libido:** Parasitic infections can lower libido in male animals, reducing mating activity.
- **Delayed Puberty:** Infestations with certain parasites can delay the onset of sexual maturity in young animals.

Gastric Signs:

- **Bloat (Ruminal Distension):** Common in cattle with gastrointestinal parasitic infections, parasites can interfere with normal digestive processes and cause bloat.
- **Gastric Ulcers:** Some parasites can lead to gastric ulcers, causing pain, decreased appetite, and weight loss in affected animals.

Hepatic Signs:

- **Liver Fluke Infection (Fasciola hepatica):** In sheep and cattle, liver fluke infections can result in liver damage, leading to signs like jaundice (yellowing of mucous membranes and skin), unthriftiness, and an enlarged liver.
- **Ascites (Abdominal Fluid Accumulation):** Liver fluke infections can lead to ascites, with a swollen, fluid-filled abdomen.

These clinical signs may vary depending on the parasite and the affected host species. Accurate diagnosis and treatment often require veterinary consultation, diagnostic testing, and management strategies specifically for parasites and livestock species.

Veterinarians will recognize these clinical signs and conduct thorough examinations to diagnose and treat underlying animal health conditions. Studying these signs leads to valuable clues and guides further diagnostic investigations.

Diagnosing Parasitic Infections

Although common clinical signs are mentioned earlier, in this section, you'll learn how to identify and diagnose them in livestock and identify examples of common parasitic infections in each species.

Common Parasitic Infections in Cattle

Gastrointestinal Nematodes:

- **Ostertagia Ostertagi (Brown Stomach Worm):** This worm primarily affects the abomasum (the fourth stomach) and can cause clinical signs such as diarrhea, weight loss, and reduced feed intake. In severe cases, it can lead to anemia due to these blood-feeding parasites.

- **Cooperia Species:** These small intestinal worms cause diarrhea, poor weight gain, and suboptimal feed utilization.

- **Haemonchus Contortus (Barber Pole Worm):** It's another blood-feeding worm that can cause severe anemia, pale mucous membranes, bottle jaw (swelling under the jaw), weight loss, and death if left untreated.

- **Liver Flukes (Fasciola Hepatica):** Liver fluke infections can reduce milk production and trigger the development of jaundice (yellowing of mucous membranes) and weight loss. They primarily affect the liver and bile ducts.

- **Lungworms (Dictyocaulus Viviparus):** Lungworm infections cause coughing, increased respiratory rate, and nasal discharge due to lung and airway damage.

- **Ticks and Mites:** External parasites like the common cattle tick (rhipicephalus (boophilus) microplus) cause skin irritation, restlessness, hair loss, and the transmission of diseases like anaplasmosis.

Recognition and Diagnosis:

- **Clinical Signs:** While it may be difficult for beginners to identify the signs, veterinarians and experienced livestock farmers can recognize parasitic infections based on observed clinical signs, including diarrhea, coughing, and skin lesions.

- **Fecal Egg Counts:** Examining fecal samples using techniques like the McMaster method to help identify the type and quantity of internal worm eggs, aiding in deworming decisions.

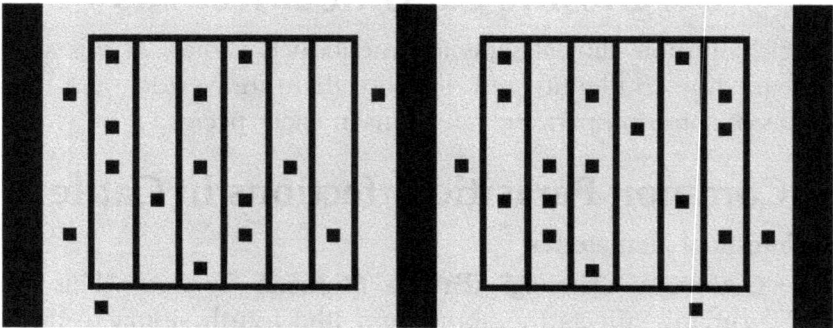

Examining fecal samples using techniques like the McMaster method to help identify the type and quantity of internal worm eggs.

- **Blood Tests:** Blood parameters indicate anemia due to blood-feeding parasites like Haemonchus contortus.

- **Physical Examination:** Veterinarians commonly conduct thorough physical examinations to identify external parasites and assess overall health.

- **Post-Mortem Examination:** In severe illness or death, necropsies (post-mortem examinations) can confirm the presence and extent of parasitic infections.

Common Parasitic Infections in Sheep and Goats

Gastrointestinal Nematodes:

- **Teladorsagia Circumcincta (Stomach Hairworm):** These worms can cause symptoms like diarrhea, weight loss, and anemia in sheep and goats.

- **Trichostrongylus Species:** Small intestinal worms lead to diarrhea, weakness, and reduced feed efficiency.
- **Nematodirus spp. (Thin-Necked Intestinal Worms):** These parasites result in diarrhea and weight loss, particularly in young animals.
- **Coccidiosis (eimeria spp.):** This protozoal infection triggers bloody diarrhea, dehydration, lethargy, and weight loss.
- **Lice and Mites:** External parasites, like the sheep keds (melophagus ovinus) and the scab mite (psoroptes ovis), cause itching, hair loss, skin lesions, and reduced productivity.

Recognition and Diagnosis:

You can do it yourself or call a veterinarian to send fecal samples to detect the presence of worm eggs and spores, conduct a thorough physical examination, and conduct relevant blood tests for appropriate recognition and diagnosis.

Common Parasitic Infections in Chickens

Internal Worms:

- **Ascarids (Roundworms):** Chickens may experience reduced weight gain, decreased egg production, and general weakness.
- **Tape Worms:** These parasites can cause poor weight gain.
- **Cecal Worms (heterakis gallinarum):** Infections with these worms result in poor growth and egg production.
- **Coccidiosis (eimeria spp.):** Chickens may develop bloody diarrhea, dehydration, lethargy, and weight loss.
- **External Parasites (e.g., mites and lice):** Feather loss, skin irritation, and reduced egg laying are common symptoms.

Examining fecal samples for parasite eggs, physical examinations, and a veterinary assessment are necessary for better intervention.

Common Parasitic Infections in Horses

Gastrointestinal Parasites:

- **Small Strongyles (cyathostomins):** These worms can cause colic, weight loss, diarrhea, and lethargy.
- **Large Strongyles (strongylus spp.):** Infections may lead to colic, unthriftiness, and, in severe cases, thromboembolic colic.

- **Ascarids (parascaris equorum):** Young horses with ascarid infections may exhibit coughing, respiratory distress, and intestinal blockages.

- **External Parasites (e.g., ticks and mites):** Restlessness, itching, skin lesions, and reduced overall health are common symptoms.

A vet assessment, fecal sample evaluation, physical examination, and blood tests are mandatory to recognize and diagnose these parasitic infections.

Remember that consulting a veterinarian is essential for accurately recognizing and diagnosing parasitic infections in livestock. Veterinarians have the expertise to interpret diagnostic results, develop treatment plans, and guide parasite control programs, ensuring the animals' health and well-being.

Diagnostic Tools

Diagnosing parasitic infections in animals involves various techniques and tools for the specific parasites and the affected species. Here are some standard diagnostic methods and tools used for identifying parasitic infections in livestock and other animals:

Fecal Egg Counts (FECs)

Fecal Egg Counts (FECs) are commonly used to diagnose parasitic infections, particularly gastrointestinal parasites like nematodes (roundworms). This technique examines animal fecal samples under a microscope to count the number of parasite eggs present. This method is non-invasive, cost-effective, and provides quantitative information about the level of infection.

FECs help veterinarians and livestock owners gauge the severity of parasitic infections, monitor the effectiveness of treatment, and make informed decisions about deworming strategies. However, it's vital to note that FECs may not detect larval or prepatent infections (infections in the early stages). Fresh fecal samples and proper laboratory techniques are essential to obtain accurate results.

Blood Tests

Blood tests are a versatile diagnostic tool for various parasitic infections. They analyze blood samples to detect specific parasite antigens or antibodies produced by the host's immune response. Blood tests can identify many parasites, including blood-borne parasites (e.g., trypanosoma) and some internal parasites.

One of the key advantages of blood tests is that the vet can detect parasitic infections even before clinical signs appear, making them valuable for early intervention. These tests can help with the diagnosis of chronic or latent infections. Specialized laboratory equipment is required to conduct blood tests, and it's not always easy to differentiate between current and past infections in some cases.

Skin Scrapings and Biopsies

Skin scrapings and biopsies are used to diagnose parasitic infections affecting the skin or skin-dwelling parasites like mites and lice. This method collects samples from affected skin areas and is examined under a microscope.

Skin scrapings and biopsies are a direct and accurate method for diagnosing ectoparasitic infestations and skin conditions. This technique requires expertise to collect and interpret samples correctly. It may also miss deep-seated parasites that are not accessible through scraping.

Necropsy

Necropsy, or post-mortem examination, entails the thorough examination of deceased animals to identify internal parasites and understand the impact of these parasites on the animal's health. This method is beneficial for diagnosing internal parasitic infections, including liver flukes.

Necropsy offers a definitive diagnosis of the effects of parasites on internal organs. It is crucial for research, understanding disease dynamics, and monitoring the health of a livestock population. An autopsy requires the sacrifice of the animal and does not apply to living animals.

Serologic Tests

Serologic tests involve the analysis of blood to detect specific antibodies or antigens associated with parasitic infections. These tests diagnose parasitic infections, especially those that cause chronic or latent conditions. They can also indicate exposure to specific parasites. Serologic tests help diagnose chronic or latent infections that other methods may not detect. The interpretation of serologic results can be complex, and the presence of antibodies does not necessarily mean an active infection. Furthermore, the test results may vary depending on the stage of the infection.

PCR (Polymerase Chain Reaction)

Polymerase Chain Reaction (PCR) is a molecular diagnostic technique that amplifies and detects parasite DNA or RNA. It is a highly sensitive and specific method capable of identifying various parasites, including protozoa and certain helminths (worms). PCR offers the advantage of high sensitivity, capable of detecting low-level infections. It is advantageous in cases where other diagnostic methods have failed. However, it requires specialized laboratory equipment and expertise, making it less accessible in some settings.

Ultrasound Imaging

Ultrasound imaging involves using sound waves to visualize internal structures in the body, helping to identify organ-specific parasitic infections. It is frequently used for diagnosing liver flukes and other internal parasites that affect organs. Ultrasound is a non-invasive and real-time imaging method that provides valuable information on organ health and any potential damage or lesions caused by parasites. Carrying out ultrasound imaging requires specialized equipment and training, and it may not detect small or early-stage infections.

Ultrasound is a non-invasive and real-time imaging method that provides valuable information on organ health and any potential damage or lesions caused by parasites.

Langgeng Anggitobumi, CC BY-SA 4.0 <https://creativecommons.org/licenses/by-sa/4.0>, via Wikimedia Commons: https://commons.wikimedia.org/wiki/File:USG_Pada_sapi_Bali.jpg

Skin Swabs and Impressions

Skin swabs and impressions are simple and non-invasive techniques used to collect samples from affected skin areas in animals. These samples are then examined to detect ectoparasites or skin conditions. It's a simple and convenient method that can be performed in the field without requiring specialized equipment. Although skin swabs reveal insights into external parasite infestations, they cannot detect all skin parasites or infections, particularly deep-seated parasites inaccessible through swabbing.

Fecal Floatation

Fecal floatation is a technique used to diagnose animal parasitic infections by examining fecal samples. In this method, the samples are mixed with a flotation solution, causing parasite eggs or cysts to float to the surface, where they can be observed under a microscope. It's a cost-effective method for detecting certain parasites, particularly protozoa and some helminths. It helps identify specific types of parasites and assess the severity of infections.

Histopathology

Histopathology involves the examination of tissue samples under a microscope to identify tissue-dwelling parasites or assess the extent of tissue damage caused by parasitic infections. This method is handy for diagnosing parasites that affect organs or tissues.

Histopathology reveals detailed information about tissue damage and the location of parasites within the affected tissue. It also requires specialized laboratory equipment and expertise for proper sample collection, processing, and interpretation.

Each diagnostic method plays a critical role in identifying parasitic infections in animals. The choice of method depends on the type of parasite, the affected organ system, the animal species, and the case's specific circumstances. Veterinarians and parasitologists use these tools to diagnose infections and develop appropriate treatments accurately.

Handling Samples for Testing

Proper sample collection, storage, and transport are essential to ensure the reliability of the results. Here are guidelines for collecting and handling samples for different diagnostic tests, along with the importance of proper storage and transport:

Fecal Samples (Fecal Egg Counts, Fecal Floatation)
Collection
- Use clean, uncontaminated containers for sample collection.
- Collect fresh fecal samples directly from the rectum or immediately after defecation.
- Ensure that the sample represents the animal's condition and collect enough to perform multiple tests if necessary.

Handling
- Label the sample container with the animal's identification and date of collection.
- Store the sample in a cool, dry place, away from direct sunlight, and seal it to prevent dehydration.
- Avoid contamination from soil or bedding material.

Transport
For fecal egg counts, transport the sample to a laboratory or veterinary clinic as soon as possible. If a delay is expected, store the sample in a refrigerator (4°C), but avoid freezing it, as freezing can damage parasite eggs.

Blood Samples (Blood Tests, Serologic Tests)
Collection
- Use sterile, vacuum-sealed blood collection tubes or syringes.
- Collect blood from a suitable vein, following aseptic techniques.
- Label the sample container with the animal's identification and date of collection.

Handling
- Allow the blood to clot by leaving the sample undisturbed at room temperature for 30-60 minutes.
- Centrifuge the sample to separate serum from clotted blood.
- Transfer the serum to a clean, labeled tube, avoiding contamination.

Storage
- Store the serum sample in a refrigerator (4°C) to prevent degradation.

- Avoid repeated freezing and thawing, which can affect the sample's integrity.

Transport

Transport the serum sample to the laboratory in a leak-proof container, maintaining a cold chain (use ice packs or coolers if necessary) to prevent temperature fluctuations.

Skin Scrapings and Biopsies
Collection

- Collect samples from affected skin areas using a sterile scalpel blade or similar instrument.
- Ensure the samples include the epidermis and any suspected parasites or skin lesions.

Handling

- Place the collected samples in a labeled container, ensuring no cross-contamination.
- Fixative solutions (e.g., 10% formalin) may be used to preserve samples for histopathology.

Storage

Store fixed samples in a cool, dark place, or refrigerate them per specific test requirements.

Transport

Transport the samples to the laboratory in a sealed, leak-proof container, ensuring the sample's integrity is preserved during transport.

Necropsy Samples
Collection

- A qualified veterinarian or pathologist should perform necropsies.
- Collect representative samples of affected tissues or organs, ensuring proper labeling and documentation.

Handling

- Keep the samples separate and well-labeled to avoid cross-contamination.
- Handle samples with care to preserve their integrity.

Storage

- Preserve tissue samples in formalin or other appropriate fixatives.

- Keep samples cool and protected from contamination before they can be transported.

Transport

Transport samples to a diagnostic laboratory, following the laboratory's specific requirements for packaging and shipping.

Proper sample handling, storage, and transport are crucial for obtaining accurate diagnostic results. Failure to adhere to these guidelines leads to sample degradation, contamination, or unreliable test outcomes. Consult with a veterinarian or diagnostic laboratory for specific diagnostic tests and sample type requirements when in doubt.

Chapter 3: Choosing the Right Natural Methods

Using natural parasite control methods for healthy herds can be difficult because they break the accepted norm. Therefore, it can be challenging to receive the correct information and advice. People have become accustomed to using the recommended over-the-counter chemical solutions. There are many benefits to exploring natural pathways to eradicate parasites and deworm your animals. Although the traditional chemical methods are working for now, some parasites are already adapting by becoming resistant to commonly used commercial dewormers. Therefore, the need for finding alternates as the traditionally used chemical options become ineffective is increasing exponentially. Moreover, the environmental impact of pharmaceutical production and transportation is antithetical to running a sustainable farm.

The wide range of animals and species-specific parasite relationships makes it difficult to apply general care. Equipping yourself with the appropriate knowledge unlocks a new world of sustainable treatment of your livestock. Grabbing hold of natural remedies for parasites opens the door to an ancient tradition that has built up tried and tested systems for centuries. Using plants and herbs for parasite control is a practice found around the world. Ancient Nordic cultures brewed carefully mixed plant medicines for their livestock, and people still report the effectiveness of these methods in these regions.

Using plants and herbs for parasite control is a practice found around the world.
https://www.pickpik.com/herbs-french-bouquet-gourmet-cuisine-rosemary-38483

As the movement for more sustainable practices grows, there will be a higher demand for remedies coming from local geographical areas. The rising environmental consciousness among many farmers has generated the development of parasite control using ingredients from their local region. Therefore, the research on natural deworming and parasite control is steadily growing. By accessing what is known and refining it to your needs, the animals you are raising, and the environmental factors unique to your ecosystem, you can extract all the benefits from natural remedies while minimizing their downsides.

Natural Deworming and Parasite Control

Natural deworming and parasite control is the use of herbal and plant solutions to treat your livestock as opposed to pharmaceutical medications that can be bought over the counter or acquired from a veterinarian. Someone motivated to use natural deworming options could be pursuing this way for numerous reasons, including parasite resistance being detected and wanting to be more eco-friendly in their farming approaches. Natural parasite management is linked to an entire philosophy that emphasizes working within the conditions of local habitats to achieve your desired farming outcomes. Following the guidelines of natural deworming is a regenerative practice that promotes mutually beneficial bonds between nature, yourself, and your livestock.

When people think of breeding organic livestock, the first thing that often comes to mind is the use of antibiotics. The development of antibiotic-resistant bugs caused many farmers to opt for the organic route. However, with the focus on the negative results of overusing antibiotics, natural antiparasitic medications (called *anthelmintics)* were overlooked. To be truly organic and reconnect with nature and healing means a complete overhaul of how you treat and maintain your livestock must be conducted. Natural deworming is not as simple as popping a few tablets in your feed. You must consider what you plant in your pasture and how your food chain connects at the micro and macro levels. By being observant and aware, you better understand the complex natural networks that result in healthy livestock.

When you look at your farm as an interdependent ecosystem and why organisms interact in mutually beneficial or hostile ways, you start to see the bigger picture of parasite management. Chemical dewormers are too narrow in their focus because they zoom into the parasite as a problem for the animal instead of viewing the broader scope of the environment. The animals you choose to keep, the pastures you plant, how you manage them, and the cleanliness of your farm all play a role in creating a situation where parasites thrive or where they are kept down to manageable rates.

When you use natural antiparasitic methods, you have to be more present in the existence of your livestock. Animals affected by parasites will behave differently and show signs of needing deworming. You also need to pick up if your pasture environment is geared toward being a breeding ground for parasites. Being able to observe these nuances comes with careful education and practice. Adopting natural ways to eliminate parasites requires a lifestyle shift because your farm or homestead needs to be restructured following the holistic approach nature demands.

Parasite management is more than a visit to the vet. You must understand both the life cycles of the animals you farm, how different species relate to one another, and the life cycles and functioning of parasitic organisms. A parasite may live inside an animal for some of its life and get transferred to the next stage through fecal matter. Once you integrate natural parasite control into your routines, you'll notice that the methods encourage biodiversity, and sourcing what you use locally positively contributes to the regeneration of the environment. From the people who consume meat to the plants, animals, and farmers – all benefit from your commitment to transitioning to using homegrown natural remedies and techniques to eliminate parasites.

Why Choose Natural Methods over Artificial Chemicals

There are pros and cons to using natural antiparasitic techniques and artificial chemicals. When you weigh up both of these methods, the natural way comes out far ahead of anything chemical on the market for many reasons. When you examine which is better, the naturalistic approach or chemical treatment, you must first explore the relationship between animals and parasites. The first point to note is realizing that every farm has parasites on it, so there is no running away from the fact that your livestock will be affected at some stage. The key to parasite management is minimizing the impact on your herd by reducing the number of affected animals and treating the ones that have already been infected.

The main attraction to using chemical antiparasitic medicine is the convenience. Once you know what parasite affects your herd, you go to the supplier and buy what you need. If a vet visits your farm, they tell you which product you need and how to use it. However, the convenience of using these pharmaceutical chemicals has caused many large-scale commercial farms to use chemicals over natural methods. This widespread use has made some parasite species immune to commonly used medicines. Some dewormers will have to be phased out because of the rising resistance to the medication. When parasites are expelled using chemical means, some of them survive. With their stronger genetics, the surviving parasites reproduce, birthing a new generation of pests immune to the chemicals that killed off the rest of their kind. Natural methods do not have the same side effects.

Other than developing super parasites resistant to dewormers, natural antiparasitic measures require you to adapt to more environmentally friendly farming methods. Since you are no longer using chemical dewormers, your animals will be unable to survive in the same conditions they once did. On inorganic farms, animals live on top of one another and are simply injected with all kinds of artificial medicine to avoid the spread of diseases and parasites that thrive in these cramp conditions. One tenet of natural parasite management is providing enough space and appropriate living conditions that are not a breeding ground for the killer critters. When you use pasture grounds and allow animals to roam in free space, they have a better quality of life. Therefore, natural parasite control is better for your livestock based on their comfort.

Dewormers can adversely impact the ecosystem, inadvertently killing creatures that work for the benefit of your farm. Chemical antiparasitic medicine may get rid of the parasites, but some of the artificial compounds are released in your livestock excrement. This penetrates the soil and kills organisms central to the environment's biodiversity and function. For example, dung beetles and earthworms could be mistakenly killed by dewormers, which will reduce the quality of your soil. The knock-on effect is that low-quality soil will then affect the crops you can grow, as well as your grazing pastures for your livestock, which means your animals will get low-quality feed. This impacts their muscle development and the birthrate of breeding animals. Farmers in Scotland started experiencing problems with the sheep herds due to the impact of dewormers on the soil. It was suggested that they reduce their use of dewormers or cease altogether. Some farmers in the region took a more targeted approach by treating only affected animals. Natural methods offer the perfect solution to the soil degradation problem.

Considerations to Make before Pursuing Natural Parasite Management

Transitioning from chemical antiparasitic solutions to natural ones can take a lot, especially at first. Each farm and set of circumstances is different, and much like nature adjusts, your approach to parasite control will shift. The livestock species, your region, and the parasites your animals are most affected by will all play a role in what techniques you implement. Jumping in head first can be tempting, especially if you are excited to explore this fulfilling journey. However, for your safety and the well-being of your animals, you need to slow down and conduct a thorough analysis of your farm. Making a few basic considerations that will affect how you approach natural deworming will increase your chances of success and avoid devasting failures that can cost you a large chunk of your herd.

Parasite Species

Parasites take many shapes and forms. For example, parasites can live inside an animal's gut, like many worm species, or on the skin's surface, like fleas and ticks. Each body part and organ of your livestock can be affected by parasitic species. Therefore, before you plan to reduce parasites, you must know which species you are dealing with and what your livestock is particularly susceptible to. Some of the parasite groups common to the geographical location that you should research are endoparasites that live inside the host, ectoparasites that live in their bodies, hemoparasites that are in the blood, or even protozoa which are unicellular microscopic parasites.

Livestock Species

The types of livestock on your farm will shape your choices for parasite control. For example, sheep and cows do not share the same parasites, but goats and sheep have some common parasites. Therefore, you must consider which animals you keep and how you raise them to prevent the spread of different parasite species. For example, grazing animals will often get reinfected with parasites because they are exposed to them more when they go out into a pasture. Keeping your grass long is one way to reduce infection rates with grazing livestock. Many parasite species only exist on the first couple of inches of grass. So, if your grass is long, your livestock will mostly eat the upper levels where there are fewer parasitic species.

Environmental Conditions

The habitat conditions your animals live in will determine which kinds of parasites develop. For example, after floods, there is usually an upsurge in parasites. Warm, wet areas will have particular parasite species that differ from desert climates. Furthermore, the hygiene conditions on your farm will also impact which parasites are around. For example, some farms keep chickens in battery cages, so they are constantly surrounded by fecal matter, which means they easily pick up parasites.

Diseases and Illnesses

Certain of your livestock will be more susceptible to dying from parasite infections due to pre-existing health issues. One of the natural ways to combat parasites is by selectively breeding your livestock. If a parasite infection spreads through your herd, separate the ones that seem the least affected and breed them. Their genetics will act as the first barrier against the negative impact of parasites. Younger animals are also usually more likely to die from parasites. Therefore, you must be mindful of the life stages of your livestock, common parasites that affect them, and what illnesses leave your herd immunocompromised. For example, you may want to keep animals recovering from certain illnesses separated from the herd to avoid infection while they are in a vulnerable state.

Proactivity and Communication with Medical Professionals

You need to consult medical professionals for effective parasite treatment and eradication, whether chemical or natural. Being proactive in contacting the vet requires you to be aware of some of the telltale signs that you have an infected herd. Different animals express illness differently when parasites infect them. Some key tips to remember are to check their energy levels, check their excrement for eggs, and examine their skin to see if there are wounds or rashes that parasitic infections can cause. If you identify one animal with worms or other parasites, it is likely that more animals in your herd are also affected. Separating affected animals is one of the first steps you should take before calling a veterinarian.

Sometimes, it is almost impossible to tell if an animal has parasites. For example, cattle with small intestinal worms and brown stomach worms show no signs of infection until the worm load is so high that it causes sudden death. When you have mysterious deaths on your farm and your animals seem otherwise healthy, it may indicate that you need to take some steps for parasite control. Calling the vet to look at the animal and the environment will help you know which parasite you are dealing with. The tests that vets run are more accurate than your calculated guesses. Even if you opt not to use the chemical pharmaceuticals vets recommend, the information they give you will guide you on what natural measures to take. If you openly communicate with your vet that you are using natural antiparasitic techniques, they can also advise you on what natural measure you should take.

An informed opinion is essential for making choices that will benefit you and your animals. Building a relationship with your vet allows you to reach out when you have concerns, and your proactivity includes your vet in advising you on your goals for animal health. Monitoring your animals closely allows you to notice anomalies earlier to catch any problem and have a better chance of catching it. Furthermore, since prevention is better than a cure, your vet will tell you what to do so your livestock is not susceptible to diseases or parasites.

You should schedule regular health checks for your herd by your veterinarian and not only rely on them for emergencies. Vets can advise you on the environmental conditions on your farm, the nutrition of your animals, as well as what medical interventions are required for your herd. Animals on a farm require constant care, and if you want to maintain or grow the numbers of your herd, it is crucial to know what is going on with their health. Therefore, proactivity in contacting your vet for regular checkups will benefit you in the long run.

A strong relationship with your vet as a team member enhances your farm in many ways. Think about going to the dentist. If you get a check-up every six months, you can address the small problems that arise along the way, and the dentist will tell you where you are going wrong in caring for your teeth. However, going to the dentist only when you have a toothache will cost you a lot more. Similarly, calling your vet occasionally will result in them participating in disaster management instead of playing their role to elevate your farm. Just like cleaning, feeding, and rotating animals on your pastures are part of your maintenance routine, veterinarian visits should be included in that list for an elite farm environment to be created that can facilitate natural antiparasitic protocols.

Creating a Deworming Plan

Having a planned schedule, as opposed to leaving deworming to the times when your livestock is already infected, is part of farming best practices. Your deworming plan, especially if you do it naturally, is about keeping a healthy, productive farm running. For example, if you have a variety of animals on your farm, you can allow your sheep and horses to graze together, but you should prevent your sheep and cattle from mixing due to cow parasites having deadly impacts on sheep herds. In this way, you can prevent using excessive deworming products, even if they are plant-based and herbal.

Goals

Your goals, as they relate to parasites, should be realistic. For example, completely eradicating all worms, ticks, or flies is impossible to achieve. Set measurable goals that are achievable and realistic. Making year-over-year comparisons will help you craft the goals to achieve with your deworming strategy. So, if you lost a certain amount of livestock to parasites the previous year, you can set a goal to lose fewer animals this year. Other goals can be related to how you organize your farm or, if you've been using chemical deworming methods, how to transition to natural options.

Needs

Every farm has individual needs depending on where it is situated and what combination of animals are being kept. For a plan to be effective, list every animal you have and the parasites that affect those animals in your location. Next, you must survey your land to see how you can best accommodate all your animals and which grazing patterns you can use to minimize their risk of getting parasites. Lastly, you must find which plants, herbs, and foods help the animals expel parasites in the numerous forms they take. Finally, you must set up emergency protocols for quarantining your livestock when necessary.

Time Management

Your daily schedule must be set by the hour so that you can do all the cleaning, culling, breeding, isolating, and feeding activities needed to keep parasites at a minimum in your herd. Remember that you must always check your animals and their excrement for signs of parasites, which takes significant time out of your day. To prevent you from feeling overwhelmed, managing your time well and scheduling every activity you must complete for the day, month, week, and season is best.

Environmental Factors

Different weather patterns and seasons bring parasites along with them. Furthermore, the habitat where you raise your animals also has an ecosystem where parasites slip neatly into the food chain. You have to draft measures to accommodate these factors. For example, after floods, stable flies are common. Therefore, you must have a preparation plan that expects this increase after the rainy season. Your animals live in tune with nature, which does not always mean positive outcomes. Nature often means suffering for animals in many cases. Therefore, you must understand the natural world around your farm to respond to it efficiently and promptly.

Chapter 4: Grazing the Parasites Away – Pasture Management

In sustainable livestock farming, one of the biggest challenges is dealing with parasites lurking in your pastures. To tackle this issue, you need a well-thought-out pasture rotation system, regardless of whether you're raising one type of animal, a mix of species, or using a specific grazing method. This system is all about controlling how long animals graze in a given area and managing their grazing habits.

A remarkable and intricate countdown begins once the parasite eggs are expelled from the host and deposited in feces. The eggs hatch within one to 14 days, usually around five days. After hatching, some parasite larvae can hang around for up to 40 days if the conditions are right – think moist and warm ground. But after about 55 days, most of these larvae will be gone unless they find a new host before that.

Knowing how parasites work can help you plan your grazing strategy to prevent your animals from getting reinfected. For example, in just four days, the notorious barber pole worm, which can harm goats and sheep, can hatch and pose a threat. Since these larvae only survive on the ground for about four weeks, it's smart to move your goats or sheep to fresh grazing areas every four days or even more often when parasite levels are high. After this intense grazing period, let those sections of pasture rest from goat or sheep grazing for at least 60 days to ensure all parasite larvae are gone. You can do this by dividing your pastures using temporary or electric fencing.

Pasture management is a great way to deal with parasites. As you learn more about pasture management, you'll discover different strategies and techniques that protect your animals from parasites and help you create a sustainable and healthy grazing routine.

Grazing as a Natural Approach to Parasite Management

Grazing in Parasite Control is a natural approach to managing and minimizing parasitic infections in livestock. It involves strategically controlling the movement and grazing patterns of animals on pasturelands to disrupt the life cycles of common livestock parasites, including nematodes (worms), coccidia, and other harmful microorganisms. Some of the different approaches you can take are set out here:

1. Strategic Grazing

Grazing in parasite control encompasses carefully planned rotation and pasture allocation. The key idea is to avoid overgrazing in one area and to give your pastures adequate resting periods, which is essential in breaking the parasite life cycle.

The key idea is to avoid overgrazing in one area and to give your pastures adequate resting periods, which is essential in breaking the parasite life cycle.
https://pixabay.com/photos/cow-grassland-grazing-nomad-7200409/

2. Rotation and Rest

This approach involves rotating animals through different pastures and allowing previously grazed areas to rest. During the resting period, the absence of host animals interrupts the completion of parasite life cycles, resulting in a decline in the overall parasite burden.

3. Controlled Grazing Intensity

Grazing intensity and duration are managed to ensure that animals do not have prolonged exposure to parasite-infested pastures. By reducing the time animals spend in a particular area and then moving them to fresh pastures, the risk of reinfection by parasites significantly decreases.

Understanding the Life Cycles of Parasites

To manage and control parasites in livestock effectively, it's essential to grasp the intricacies of their life cycles. Different parasites, such as nematodes and coccidia, have specific life stages and dependencies on environmental conditions. Understanding these life cycles is key to developing successful parasite control strategies. For instance, the barber pole worm (haemonchus contortus) affects small ruminants like goats and sheep. Its life cycle involves egg shedding in the host, hatching into larvae that develop in pasture, and reinfection of the host through ingesting infective larvae. Recognizing this cycle is vital to addressing barber pole worm infestations.

Grazing management is an effective tool for interrupting the life cycles of common livestock parasites. By putting well-planned rotational grazing and pasture rest periods in place, you can break the chain of infection. Through rotation, you move livestock to different pastures. During the resting phase, the absence of host animals prevents the completion of parasite life cycles. For example, the larvae shed in feces require host contact to develop into adult worms. Consider a rotation cycle that moves goats to a new pasture every 35 days. This allows the previously grazed pastures to rest for at least 60 days. During this period, the majority of parasite larvae will perish.

Controlling grazing intensity and duration is essential. Limiting animals' time on a particular pasture and then relocating them to fresh ones reduces the risk of reinfection. Rapid movement to new pastures prevents animals from consuming infective larvae lingering in their previous grazing areas. If you have a high-risk parasite like the barber pole worm, you may have to move goats every four days during peak infestation periods, preventing larvae from becoming infective.

Grazing Strategies

1. Custom Grazing Habits

When designing a rotation system, pay attention to your livestock's specific habits and needs. Different species have unique preferences, and tailoring your grazing practices to their behavior can be highly effective. For instance, if you consider goats and cattle, goats are browsers and prefer various forage types, while cattle are primarily grazers and focus on grass. Consider this when planning which pastures to allocate for each species to maximize their nutrition intake and minimize parasite exposure.

2. Pasture Orientation

The orientation of pastures also plays a role in parasite control. You will notice that the larvae dry out faster on your south-facing slopes than in other pastures, particularly during spring. The combination of sun and slope reduces moisture and larval survival. If you have a south-facing pasture available, reserve it for use in spring when moisture levels in the soil and grass are higher. This combination promotes rapid larval desiccation, decreasing the risk of livestock ingesting infective larvae.

3. Understanding Larvae Movement

Recognizing how larvae behave in different conditions is crucial. Wet grass encourages larvae to move away from feces, while dry conditions keep them closer to the ground. Understanding these patterns helps you to determine your grazing strategies. For instance, in wet conditions, larvae may be found up to a foot away from feces, making it important to move livestock frequently to prevent ingestion. In dry conditions, larvae stay closer to the ground, reducing the risk of consumption.

4. Impact of Weather

Weather conditions can influence parasite larvae behavior. Larvae tend to climb higher on plants during overcast periods, like rainy days or early mornings and late afternoons, to avoid bright light. Being aware of these conditions helps in managing grazing schedules. Avoid grazing livestock during early mornings or late afternoons on overcast days or right after rain, as this is when larvae are more likely to be higher on plants. Instead, plan grazing sessions for drier and brighter periods.

5. Electric Fencing

Implementing one or two strands of electric fencing is a practical way to divide pastures into sections. This approach enables you to move livestock frequently, control their access, and prevent overgrazing. Create temporary sections within your pasture using electric fencing. After a certain period, move livestock to the next section, allowing the previous one to rest. This not only controls parasite infection but also optimizes forage utilization.

Seasonal Pasture Management

Seasonal pasture management involves tailoring your grazing practices to leverage the changing conditions and particular requirements of each season to maximize livestock nutrition and effectively disrupt parasite life cycles. In this approach, the seasonal rotation of livestock is guided by the conditions of the time of year. Whether you are taking advantage of the warming spring sun to desiccate parasite larvae or utilizing lush summer pastures to limit parasite exposure, these strategies aim to promote both the well-being of your livestock and the control of parasitic burdens.

1. Spring Pasture

During spring, focus on pastures that face south and have a sloping terrain. These features maximize sun exposure and efficient drying of the pasture. As a result, it reduces moisture levels, which is critical for parasite larvae survival. For example, a south-facing pasture with good sun exposure helps dry feces and the surrounding soil, decreasing the likelihood of larvae survival. Grazing in such pastures during this season can help control parasite infestation.

2. Summer Pasture

In hot summer months, lowland grazing areas with lush vegetation are advantageous. The heat forces parasite larvae to stay closer to the ground and moist manure, making them less likely to be consumed by grazing animals. Summer pastures in lowland areas with ample grass growth are ideal. As the sun intensifies, larvae remain close to the ground, reducing the risk of livestock ingesting them.

3. Fall Pasture

In the fall, diversify your livestock's diet by offering nuts, fruits, and leaves. However, monitor moisture levels and temperatures, as some parasites can survive under leaf cover. Goats, sheep, and other livestock species can benefit from the nutritional variety provided by these additions to their diet. Be cautious and monitor weather conditions to ensure that parasite survival is minimized.

4. Winter Pasture

Winter pastures in regions with USDA Hardiness Zones of 6 or higher can include taller, "stocked" forage. The cold winter conditions naturally reduce parasite populations. Utilize winter pastures with taller forage growth. The combination of cold temperatures in Zone 6 or higher and the absence of hosts on the pasture helps decrease parasite burdens during the winter months.

Other Grazing Methods

1. Multi-Species Grazing

Multi-species grazing, especially during heavy growth periods, can be a powerful tool to prevent overgrazing and reinfection. When different livestock species graze together, they have varying preferences for forage types and different grazing habits, reducing the pressure on specific plants and mitigating the risk of parasite transmission. For example, combining cattle and goats in a multi-species grazing system can be very effective. Cattle primarily graze grasses, while goats are browsers and prefer shrubs and forbs. This diversity in grazing behavior can help minimize the impact on any single forage type.

2. Mixed Livestock Grazing

Mixed livestock grazing involves combining different species on the same pasture, such as cattle and goats or horses and sheep. However, it's crucial to avoid grazing sheep and goats in succession since they share many parasite species, and consecutive grazing can lead to increased parasite burdens. Grazing cattle and horses together is an option, as their dietary preferences and digestive systems complement each other. Cattle primarily graze grasses, while horses are more selective, often avoiding certain grass species. This combination can lead to more efficient forage utilization.

3. Timing Is Crucial

Timing is essential when moving livestock back onto pastures, particularly during wet conditions. Rushing livestock back before 60 days have passed can lead to increased parasite levels. Instead, schedule grazing during dry, bright daylight hours to minimize exposure to infective larvae. During wet seasons or in rainy areas, ensure that pastures have adequate time to rest between grazing sessions. Grazing during dry, sunny hours when the grass and ground are less likely to harbor infective larvae is prudent.

Grazing during dry, sunny hours when the grass and ground are less likely to harbor infective larvae is prudent.

https://www.rawpixel.com/image/3260248/free-photo-image-livestock-farm-calf-yard

4. Grazing Height

Maintaining the ideal grass height is crucial for both optimal forage quality and effective parasite control. Aim to keep the grass between 6 to 8 inches in height. Grass that is too short makes it easier for livestock to ingest infective larvae, while excessively tall grass limits eggs and larvae from being dried out by sunlight. Regularly measure the grass height in your pastures to ensure it falls within the 6 to 8-inch range. This promotes better forage utilization and limits parasite exposure by keeping the grass at an ideal height.

Beneficial Soil Organisms

1. Predatory Nematodes

Predatory nematodes are microscopic worms that play a crucial role in reducing parasite populations. These nematodes are natural predators of parasite eggs and larvae, effectively controlling their numbers. For instance, consider Steinernema carpocapsae, a predatory nematode species highly effective against various parasite larvae, including houseflies, stable flies, and flea larvae. You can significantly reduce parasite levels by releasing these nematodes into your pastures.

2. Beneficial Beetles

Beneficial beetles, including ground beetles, rove beetles, and dung beetles, are essential components of a healthy pasture ecosystem. They help control parasite larvae and contribute to improved soil and plant health. Dung beetles are particularly valuable for parasite control. There are three types of dung beetles: rollers/tumblers, tunnelers, and dwellers. Rollers and tunnelers bury manure beneath the ground, effectively trapping parasite eggs and larvae. This not only prevents hatching but also improves soil and plant health.

Dung beetles, especially the tumblers and tunnelers, significantly impact parasite control. They work diligently to bury livestock manure, ensuring parasite eggs and larvae are too deep within the soil to reach the surface. As dung beetles bury manure, they also bury any parasite eggs and larvae present in the feces. This disrupts the life cycle of parasites and promotes the drying and deactivation of eggs and larvae, reducing their infectivity.

3. Scattered Manure

Due to dung beetle activity or other factors, scattered manure dries more quickly than clumped or concentrated manure. The quicker drying process shortens the opportunity for parasite larvae to remain moist and infectious. In pastures with active dung beetle populations or efficient manure scattering, you'll notice that manure is dispersed across the pasture. This scattered manure dries rapidly, making it an inhospitable environment for parasite larvae.

Environmental Control

You can implement measures to control deer access to pastures, especially those designated as harmful to goats, sheep, llamas, alpacas, and calves. Deer can serve as hosts for certain parasites and add to the contamination of pastures. Use top-strand electric fencing or guardian dogs to deter deer from grazing in pastures. Limiting deer access reduces the risk of parasite transmission to your animals.

You can also use fowl, like ducks, chickens, and other poultry, to manage gastropods, which are intermediate hosts for various parasites. Fowl can help control snail and slug populations, reducing the risk of livestock ingesting these parasites. You can allow ducks and chickens to forage in pastures prone to gastropod infestations. Their natural behavior of pecking at snails and slugs limits the numbers of these intermediate hosts, contributing to reduced parasite burdens in your livestock.

Environmental Maintenance

Effective environmental maintenance is key to managing parasite infections in livestock and promoting overall farm health. Consider the following steps to create a conducive environment that discourages parasites and supports beneficial organisms:

1. Reduce Close-Cut Mowing and Excessive Sun Exposure

Moisture-dependent organisms, like predatory nematodes and dung beetles, require some shade to thrive. Avoid close-cut mowing and extended exposure to constant sunlight, which creates ideal conditions for these beneficial organisms. A balance between sun and shade allows for the coexistence of these organisms and reduces the potential for parasite contamination. So, maintain a mixture of shaded and sunny areas within your pastures to support the activity of moisture-dependent organisms.

2. Avoid Chemical Usage

Refrain from using chemical dewormers, herbicides, pesticides, and other chemical compounds in your pastures. Chemical substances can disrupt the life cycles of beneficial organisms, reducing their effectiveness in parasite control. Choose natural and organic alternatives to minimize the harm to these beneficial creatures. This practice helps to preserve the populations of predatory nematodes, dung beetles, and other beneficial soil organisms.

3. Promote Clean Water Systems

Keep control of clean and efficient water systems for your livestock by eliminating standing water puddles. Stagnant water is a breeding ground for parasites and protozoa, increasing the risk of infection. Encourage livestock to drink from clean, regularly maintained water tanks. When implementing rotational grazing, use movable tanks with floats that can be easily moved from section to section. Regular cleaning and filling of these tanks ensure that livestock have access to clean water, reducing the risk of waterborne parasite infections.

4. Keep High-Traffic Areas Clean

Regularly clean and maintain paddocks, stalls, feeding areas, and other high-traffic areas. Damp debris, like loose hay and leaves, can protect the parasites and increase the likelihood of livestock ingesting them. Keeping these areas clean and dry minimizes the risk of parasite contamination. After cleaning, apply drying agents such as barn lime, sulfur powder, wood ash, or diatomaceous earth to the surfaces. These agents help dry out any remaining parasite eggs and larvae, further reducing the risk of infection.

Including these pasture management and environmental control practices will help reduce the risk of parasite infection and ensure a healthier and more productive herd.

Limitations of Grazing-Based Parasite Control

1. Climate Variability

Climate variability can significantly influence the effectiveness of grazing-based parasite control. Different weather conditions, such as prolonged periods of rain or drought, can impact parasite survival and transmission. It's essential to consider these challenges and adapt your grazing strategies accordingly.

- **Rain and Moisture**

    Excessive rainfall and high humidity can create ideal conditions for parasite survival, making it challenging to control parasite populations. In such cases, adjusting your grazing rotations, reducing stocking rates, or implementing other parasite management techniques may be necessary.

- **Drought and Limited Forage**

    Conversely, drought conditions can limit forage availability, which might lead to overgrazing and increased parasite exposure. During droughts, you may need to provide supplemental feed and water to keep your livestock healthy and reduce the risk of parasite infection.

2. Considerations for Specific Livestock Species

    Different livestock species have varying susceptibility to parasites. Understanding your livestock's specific needs and vulnerabilities is crucial for effective parasite control.

For example, goats and sheep are more susceptible to barber pole worms, while cattle face different challenges.

- **Species-Specific Management**

  Tailor your grazing management to what your livestock needs. Consider their natural behaviors, dietary preferences, and parasite susceptibility. Implement rotational grazing that aligns with the specific requirements of each species.

- **Selective Grazing**

  Some livestock, like goats, are known for their selective grazing habits. Utilize this behavior to your advantage by planting parasite-repelling plants in their pastures, encouraging them to self-medicate.

Extra Tips for Good Pasture Management Practices

1. Soil Health and Fertility

Soil health is fundamental to pasture management as it directly impacts forage quality, livestock nutrition, and overall farm productivity. Implement practices to improve and maintain soil fertility.

- **Soil Testing**: Conduct regular soil tests to assess nutrient levels, pH, and other factors. Soil testing provides essential data to guide your fertilization and liming strategies.
- **Fertilization**: Based on soil test results, apply appropriate organic or mineral fertilizers to correct nutrient imbalances and enhance soil fertility. Well-fertilized pastures support lush, nutritious forage.
- **Liming**: Adjust soil pH using agricultural lime to create a more favorable environment for nutrient uptake by forage plants.
- **Organic Matter**: Increase organic matter in the soil through composting, cover cropping, and rotational grazing practices. Higher organic matter content improves water retention, aeration, and nutrient cycling.

2. Monitoring and Record-Keeping

Effective pasture management requires regular monitoring and diligent record-keeping to make informed decisions and track changes.

- **Pasture Walks**: Schedule frequent pasture walks to assess forage growth, plant health, and any signs of overgrazing or parasite issues.
- **Record Livestock Movements**: Maintain records of livestock rotations, including dates and pastures used. This information helps prevent overgrazing and optimize parasite control.
- **Weather Observations**: Keep a weather journal to record conditions such as rainfall, temperature, and humidity. These factors influence grazing strategies and parasite activity.
- **Growth Data:** Measure and record forage height and density to determine when to rotate livestock and prevent overgrazing.

3. Forage Selection and Pasture Renovation

The selection of appropriate forage species and regular pasture renovation are key parts of maintaining productive and healthy pastures.

- **Forage Diversity**: Diversify your pasture with a mix of forage species that suit your region and livestock. Choose varieties that provide a balance of nutrition and palatability.
- **Renovation Practices**: Implement overseeding and reseeding as part of pasture renovation. These practices help introduce new, productive forage varieties and improve overall pasture quality.
- **Grazing Heights**: Set grazing heights to maintain healthy pasture plants. Avoid overgrazing, which weakens plants, and under-grazing, which allows weeds to proliferate.
- **Rotational Grazing**: Continuously rotate livestock through pastures to prevent overgrazing and allow forage to recover.

Pasture management is a cornerstone of sustainable livestock production, offering numerous benefits. It leads to improved animal health and performance through balanced nutrition and reduced parasite loads. It minimizes environmental impacts, including soil erosion and nutrient runoff, while enhancing forage production and soil health. Pasture management allows for reduced reliance on chemical dewormers and other synthetic interventions, contributing to a balanced ecosystem that supports biodiversity and beneficial organisms.

Chapter 5: Nutrition and Immunity

Nutrition and immunity in livestock are intricately connected. The quality and balance of the animals' diet are pivotal in bolstering their immune system. Essential nutrients like proteins, vitamins, and minerals are necessary for a healthy immune function. Well-nourished livestock are better equipped to resist infections, recover from illnesses, and maintain overall health than animals that are kept nutrient-deficient.

Inadequate nutrition weakens the immune response, making animals more vulnerable to diseases. Therefore, ensuring a proper and balanced diet is necessary to optimize the immune defense systems in livestock. Feeding the proper nutrients through a well-balanced diet prevents diseases, enabling them to ward off infections and remain resilient to various health challenges.

Nutrition, the immune system, and parasite control influence each other. Here's the critical link between these three factors for a clear perspective.

Nutrition and the Immune System

Proper nutrition supports the immune system's functionality. A well-nourished animal is better equipped to have an adequate immune response when exposed to pathogens, including parasites. For example, protein is essential for producing antibodies and immune cells, while vitamins and minerals play critical roles in various immune functions.

Proper nutrition supports the immune system's functionality.
https://pixabay.com/photos/goats-lambs-animal-goats-lambs-5110369/

Nutrition and Parasite Control

Although every nutrient has a role in strengthening the immune system and protecting livestock from diseases, certain nutrients like zinc and selenium directly improve the animal's resistance to parasites. The natural defense mechanism of animals weakens when some nutrients are not included in a balanced diet, increasing the chances of developing parasitic infections.

Immune System and Parasite Control

As you already know, the immune system is the first line of defense against parasites or other infectious diseases. When an animal is exposed to parasites, a properly functioning immune system can identify, attack, and control the parasites' populations within the host's body. This is particularly necessary in preventing parasitic infections from becoming severe or causing long-term health issues.

Striking a balance between adequate nutrition, caring for the immune system, and parasite control is imperative to maintain the health and productivity of the livestock. Proper nutrition supports a robust immune response, which, in turn, helps in preventing and controlling parasitic infections. Farmers and livestock managers must feed well-balanced diets, manage pasture rotation, and use appropriate veterinary treatments to ensure the health and well-being of their animals while minimizing the risk of parasitic infections.

Why Feed a Balanced Diet

Providing a balanced diet to livestock is necessary for several reasons mentioned here:

Nutrient Support

A balanced diet includes essential nutrients like proteins, carbohydrates, fats, vitamins, and minerals in appropriate proportions. Besides maintaining the functioning of the immune system and developing adequate immune responses, nutrients are required in thousands of other metabolic processes. Inadequate or imbalanced nutrition only weakens the immune system and can trigger certain medical conditions, ultimately making animals more susceptible to infections.

Energy and Maintenance

Livestock require a sufficient energy supply to keep their basic bodily functions healthy and support growth, reproduction, and milk production. A well-balanced diet ensures that animals have the energy to carry out these functions efficiently. When animals are malnourished, their energy levels drop, making them more vulnerable to diseases and less capable of maintaining their overall health.

Disease Resistance

The immune system relies on nutrients like vitamins (e.g., vitamin C, vitamin D), minerals (e.g., zinc, selenium), and proteins to function effectively. These nutrients are involved in antibody production, white blood cell activity, and other immune responses. A balanced diet ensures livestock receive the necessary building blocks to mount a robust defense against pathogens. Conversely, poor nutrition leads to immunosuppression, reducing the animal's ability to resist diseases.

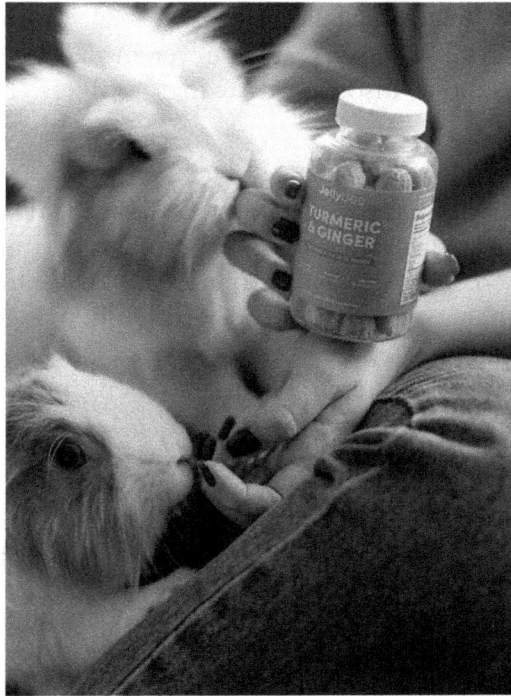

The immune system relies on nutrients like vitamins (e.g., vitamin C, vitamin D), minerals (e.g., zinc, selenium), and proteins to function effectively.

https://unsplash.com/photos/person-holding-orange-plastic-bottle-eUGppEZgkAM

Growth and Reproduction

Healthy animals are more likely to reach their growth potential and produce offspring successfully. Malnourished animals may experience growth stunts and reproductive problems, making them more susceptible to diseases due to weakened physiological states.

Maintenance of Body Condition

Adequate muscle mass is essential for locomotion and the ability to escape from disease vectors and predators. Furthermore, maintaining an appropriate body condition ensures that animals have adequate fat reserves, which can be crucial during stress, such as cold weather or disease outbreaks. The meat quality also improves when adequate nutrients are fed to the animal.

Preventing Metabolic Disorders

Certain diseases and conditions in livestock are associated with imbalances in the diet. For example, overfeeding grains to cattle can lead to conditions like acidosis, while inadequate calcium and phosphorus levels can result in disorders like milk fever in dairy cows. A balanced diet prevents metabolic disorders like these, which can harm animal health.

Resistance to Stress

Proper nutrition enhances an animal's ability to cope with various forms of discomfort, like stress and agitation, which is evident during transportation, changes in environmental conditions, and the introduction of new animals to the herd. When livestock are well-nourished, they are more resilient to stressors, which can otherwise suppress the immune system and make them more susceptible to diseases.

Lowering the Risk of Zoonotic Diseases

Balanced nutrition can also affect food safety and human health. Some diseases in livestock are zoonotic, meaning they can be transmitted to humans. Maintaining disease resistance in livestock through proper nutrition reduces the risk of zoonotic diseases, benefiting nearby animal and human populations.

Dietary Components for a Robust Immune System

The amount and type of feed change depending on the livestock type. Cattle require a mix of hay, grass, grains, silage, and legumes, whereas goats are mostly kept on dry or green forage with added protein and mineral concentrates. Here are the essential components dietary must include for adequate health and well-being.

- **Protein:** This is essential for producing antibodies, enzymes, and immune cells central to the immune response. Amino acids, the building blocks of proteins, are required for adequate immune function.
- **Vitamins:** Specific vitamins are essential for immune function, including vitamin A (for maintaining epithelial barriers), vitamin D (for regulating immune responses), and vitamin E (an antioxidant that supports immune health). Vitamin C is also essential in some livestock species.
- **Minerals:** As mentioned earlier, zinc, selenium, and copper are required for various immune functions, including producing

and adequately functioning white blood cells, acting as antioxidants, and supporting immune cell activity. Each mineral has a particular effect on the metabolism and immune activity.

- **Probiotics:** Beneficial bacteria in the digestive tract, known as probiotics, can help improve gut health and indirectly strengthen immune function by maintaining a balanced gut microbiome. A healthy gut is essential for nutrient absorption and overall well-being.

- **Prebiotics:** These are dietary components that support the growth of beneficial gut bacteria. Prebiotics, such as certain types of fiber, can enhance the effectiveness of probiotics and promote a healthy gut environment. The pro and prebiotics combine to form synbiotics. These are combinations of probiotics and prebiotics. Synbiotics can provide a dual benefit by introducing beneficial bacteria with the nourishment they need to thrive.

Omega-3 Fatty Acids: These healthy fats have anti-inflammatory properties and can support the immune system by reducing inflammation.

- **Antioxidants:** Various antioxidants, like vitamin E and others, help protect immune cells from oxidative damage and support their proper functioning.

- **Water:** Adequate hydration is essential for all physiological processes, including the immune response. Water helps transport nutrients and remove waste products, supporting overall health and immunity.

- **Carbohydrates and Energy:** Livestock require energy from carbohydrates to fuel immune responses and maintain their health. Proper energy intake is essential for immune function.

- **Herbs and Botanicals:** Some plants, herbs, and botanicals have been used in livestock diets for their potential immunomodulatory effects. These include substances like echinacea, garlic, and oregano. These herbs should always be given in minute quantities and in consultation with a certified veterinarian.

- **Immunomodulators:** Certain compounds, like β-glucans derived from yeast or algae, have been shown to augment the immune system in livestock when included in their diets.

It's necessary to note that the specific dietary requirements for a robust immune system can vary among different livestock species and individual animals. To ensure optimal immune health, it's advisable to consult with a veterinarian or animal nutritionist to formulate a diet that meets the unique needs of the livestock in question.

Nutrition Deficiencies Affecting Immune System

Deficiencies in the vital nutrients and dietary components essential for a robust immune system in livestock can compromise immune function, leading to a range of health issues and increased susceptibility to diseases.

Protein Deficiency

Animals with insufficient dietary protein may experience reduced production of antibodies and immune cells. These antibodies are essential for recognizing and neutralizing pathogens, and immune cells play a crucial role in immune responses. A protein deficiency can weaken immune responses, making animals more susceptible to diseases. Their ability to combat infections may be compromised. Furthermore, slow wound healing and impaired tissue repair can also result from protein deficiency, as these processes need proteins to produce and repair damaged tissues.

Vitamin Deficiencies

Different vitamin deficiencies have varying effects. Vitamin A deficiency can impair the integrity of epithelial barriers, such as the skin and mucous membranes, which serve as the body's first line of defense against pathogens. Weakened barriers make it easier for infectious agents to enter the body. Likewise, vitamin D deficiency leads to improper regulation of immune responses. It can potentially result in autoimmune diseases, where the immune system attacks the body's tissues. Similarly, vitamin E deficiency weakens the immune system's ability to defend against oxidative stress and infections and increases disease susceptibility.

Mineral Deficiencies

White blood cells are vital for recognizing and attacking pathogens. A zinc deficiency reduces white blood cell function and impairs immune responses. Copper deficiency can also negatively impact the development and function of immune cells. This impairs the immune system's ability to defend against pathogens.

Probiotic and Prebiotic Deficiencies

An imbalance in the gut microbiome can result from deficiencies in probiotics and prebiotics. This condition, known as gut dysbiosis, can disrupt the immune system's interaction with the gut, increase the chances of developing gut infections, and make it challenging to protect against diseases.

Omega-3 Fatty Acid Deficiency

Omega-3 fatty acids have anti-inflammatory properties. A deficiency in these healthy fats can lead to improper immune regulation, potentially causing excessive inflammation and increasing the risk of chronic diseases. Livestock with omega-3 fatty acid deficiencies may exhibit reduced resistance to infectious diseases, as inflammation is a critical component of the immune response.

Antioxidant Deficiencies

A lack of antioxidants, such as selenium and vitamin E, can increase susceptibility to oxidative stress. Oxidative stress can damage immune cells and impair their function. Livestock with antioxidant deficiencies may weaken the immune system's ability to combat infections.

Carbohydrate and Energy Deficiency

Inadequate carbohydrate and energy intake can result in reduced energy levels, which can weaken the immune response. Immune cells require energy to function effectively. Animals with energy deficiencies may experience slower recovery from illness and compromised health as their bodies struggle to mount immune responses and repair damaged tissues.

Water Deficiency

Dehydration can obstruct the transport of nutrients and the removal of waste products, impacting immune cell function and the overall health of livestock. Likewise, an increased risk of heat stress can result from water deficiency, further compromising the immune system and leading to other health problems.

Herbs, Botanicals, and Immunomodulators

The effects of specific herbs, botanicals, and immunomodulators on immune function can vary. Some may strengthen the immune system, while others may have limited or unproven effects. The absence of these dietary components means missing the potential immunomodulatory benefits they could provide to livestock, potentially affecting their immune health.

Deficiencies in these vital nutrients and dietary components can significantly affect the immune system of livestock. These effects can manifest as increased susceptibility to diseases, compromised immune responses, slower illness recovery, and impaired overall health and productivity. Therefore, proper nutrition and dietary management are essential for maintaining a strong and effective immune system in livestock.

Gut Health and Nutrition

The gut, specifically the gastrointestinal (GI) tract, is a complex and dynamic system responsible for various critical functions, and nutrition significantly influences its health.

Providing Nutrients

Nutrition supplies the energy and essential nutrients required to grow, maintain, and repair the cells lining the GI tract. The cells in the gut mucosa have a rapid turnover, and proper nutrition ensures replenishment of these cells, keeping the integrity of the gut lining true.

Promoting a Healthy Gut Microbiome

The alimentary system is home to trillions of beneficial microorganisms, including bacteria, viruses, and fungi, collectively known as the gut microbiome. A balanced diet with appropriate fibers and prebiotics can support the growth of beneficial gut bacteria. These microorganisms are crucial in digestion, nutrient absorption, and immune function. A healthy gut microbiome helps protect against harmful pathogens and contributes to overall gut health.

Maintaining Gut Barrier Function

The gut lining is a barrier that prevents the entry of harmful substances, such as pathogens and toxins, into the bloodstream. Proper nutrition supports the upkeep of a strong gut barrier by providing the necessary nutrients for mucin production and tight junction proteins. A compromised gut barrier can lead to leaky gut syndrome, allowing unwanted substances to enter the bloodstream, potentially leading to inflammation and various health issues.

Modulating Inflammation

Certain nutrients and dietary components can cause or reduce gut inflammation. Omega-3 fatty acids, for example, have anti-inflammatory properties and help manage inflammatory conditions like inflammatory bowel disease (IBD). Proper nutrition can modulate the inflammatory response in the gut and contribute to gut health.

Preventing Gastrointestinal Disorders

Nutritional choices can impact the development and progression of various gastrointestinal disorders, including conditions like gastritis, gastroenteritis, and colorectal cancer. A fiber-rich diet with fruits, vegetables, and antioxidants can reduce the risk of some GI diseases and support gut health.

Balancing Gut pH

Nutrition can influence the pH levels in the gut. An optimal pH environment is vital for adequately-functioning digestive enzymes and the gut microbiome. Ph imbalances can lead to conditions like acid reflux, which dietary choices can influence.

Supporting Gut Motility

Adequate dietary fiber and hydration are needed to support healthy gut motility. Proper movement of food and waste through the GI tract prevents constipation and ensures the efficient absorption of nutrients.

Management of Food Allergies and Intolerances

Some animals may have food allergies or intolerances that affect their gut health. Proper nutrition, which includes avoiding trigger foods, can help manage these conditions and alleviate symptoms.

Livestock Disease Influences

Mastitis (Dairy Cattle)

Proper nutrition ensures that cows have the resources needed to maintain healthy udders, which can help prevent mastitis. Furthermore, a healthy cow is likelier to have a strong defense system that can respond effectively to intruding pathogens. When mastitis does occur, a robust immune response is necessary to fight off the infection and promote recovery.

Foot and Mouth Disease (Various Livestock)

In the case of foot and mouth disease, a well-nourished animal with a sound immune response is more likely to resist the infection and recover quickly. The virus can spread more easily among animals with weakened immune systems, emphasizing the importance of nutrition in preventing and managing this highly contagious disease.

Coccidiosis (Poultry, Cattle, Sheep, and Goats)

A balanced diet that meets the nutritional needs of livestock helps prevent coccidiosis. A well-nourished animal is better equipped to mount a strong immune response against coccidial parasites.

Respiratory Diseases (Swine, Poultry, Cattle)

Nutrients, including vitamins and minerals, support lung function and can help prevent respiratory diseases. Furthermore, a healthy immune system is critical for preventing and managing infections caused by respiratory pathogens like bacteria and viruses. Livestock with compromised immune systems are more vulnerable to severe respiratory infections.

Parasitic Infections (Various Livestock)

Parasites, such as gastrointestinal worms, can be particularly detrimental to animals with compromised immune responses. Adequate provision of probiotics through nutrition is essential for controlling and limiting the impact of parasitic infections.

Clostridial Diseases (Sheep and Cattle)

Proper nutrition supports their immune system, which is necessary for preventing and managing clostridial diseases. These diseases, caused by clostridium bacteria, can be particularly severe in animals with weakened immune defenses.

Mycoplasma Infections (Poultry, Swine, Cattle)

The nutrients fed to livestock strengthen the immune system, allowing it to develop a feasible immune response that decreases the severity and the duration of infections.

Salmonellosis (Various Livestock)

A healthy gut is less susceptible to colonization by salmonella bacteria, reducing the risk of salmonellosis. In addition, a robust immune system is vital for controlling the infection and preventing its spread to other animals. Proper nutrition and a strong immune response are key factors in preventing and managing Salmonella infections.

Management Practices to Follow

Access to Clean Water

Ensure a constant supply of clean, fresh water for your livestock. Adequate hydration is essential for overall health and immune function—regularly clean water troughs and containers to prevent the growth of harmful bacteria and ensure good water quality.

Balanced Diet

Consult with a nutritionist or veterinarian to formulate a balanced diet for your livestock. Different species and life stages have unique nutritional requirements. Use high-quality, properly stored feed to ensure nutrient content and quality. Monitor feed availability, especially during extreme weather conditions, and adjust rations as needed.

Forage and Pasture Management

Practice rotational grazing to prevent overgrazing and allow pastures to recover. This approach can help maintain forage quality and reduce the risk of parasitic infections. Monitor forage quality and adjust the diet accordingly, especially during different seasons.

Vaccination and Disease Prevention

Put a vaccination program in place based on your livestock's specific disease risks. Consult with a veterinarian to develop a comprehensive vaccination schedule. You'll need proper biosecurity measures to prevent the introduction of diseases to your farm. Quarantine new animals to minimize the risk of disease transmission.

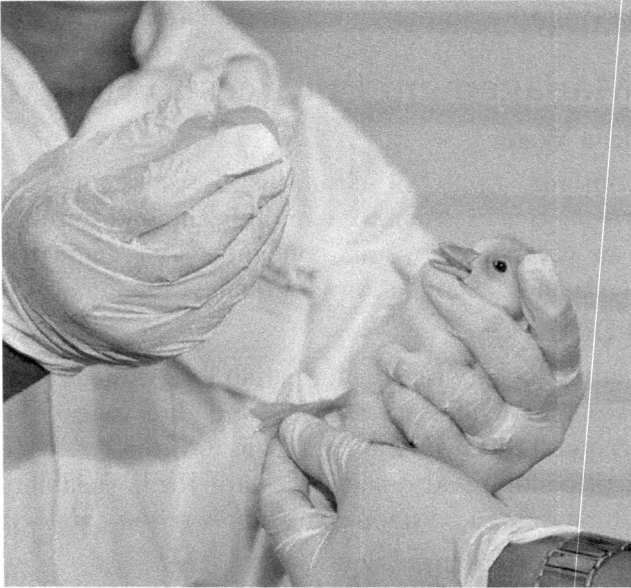

Put a vaccination program in place based on your livestock's specific disease risks.

Stress Management

Minimize stress factors such as overcrowding, abrupt changes in diet, and transportation, as these can weaken the immune system. Handle livestock gently and calmly to reduce stress during routine management practices.

Environmental Hygiene

Keep living areas clean and well-ventilated to reduce the risk of respiratory infections. Properly manage manure and waste to minimize the risk of disease vectors breeding and keep your environment clean.

Mineral and Vitamin Supplements

Test your fields and forage for mineral content to determine if supplementation is necessary. Consult a nutritionist for specific recommendations. If necessary, set up mineral blocks or supplements.

Monitoring and Record Keeping

Regularly monitor the health and condition of your livestock. Look for signs of illness or stress. Keep detailed records of vaccinations, feeding practices, and health observations to identify trends and potential issues.

Parasite Control

Develop a parasite control program that includes regular deworming and rotational grazing practices. Use fecal egg counts to monitor parasite burdens and assess the effectiveness of your parasite control program.

Genetic Selection

When choosing breeding stock, consider genetic traits related to disease resistance and overall health. Select animals with a history of strong immunity and resistance to common diseases.

Temperature and Weather Considerations

Provide adequate shelter to protect livestock from extreme weather conditions. Exposure to cold, wet, or excessively hot environments can weaken the immune system. Adjust feeding schedules and quantities in response to seasonal changes in nutritional requirements.

Consultation and Education

Work closely with veterinarians, nutritionists, and extension services to stay informed about best practices and advancements in livestock management. Regularly educate yourself and your staff on the latest research and recommendations for nutrition and health management.

A balanced diet, including adequate protein, vitamins, minerals, and essential nutrients, is fundamental for immune function and overall well-being. Proper nutrition supports a robust immune system, reducing the risk and severity of diseases.

Components like probiotics, prebiotics, and synbiotics help maintain a healthy gut microbiome, while omega-3 fatty acids, antioxidants, and carbohydrates support immune responses. Deficiencies of these vital nutrients can compromise immune function and leave livestock vulnerable to infections and health issues.

Furthermore, practical management practices play a crucial role in maintaining optimal health. These include ensuring access to clean water, rotational grazing for forage quality, vaccination and disease prevention, stress reduction, environmental hygiene, and genetic selection for disease resistance.

Monitoring, record-keeping, and consultation with veterinarians and nutritionists are also vital. By incorporating these measures into livestock management, you can help ensure that your animals receive the right nutrition, maintain strong immune systems, and are better equipped to resist diseases, ultimately optimizing their overall health and productivity.

Chapter 6: Herbal Remedies

It is never easy seeing your livestock infected with parasites. Naturally, you want to find the best remedy for them, but traditional medicine contains chemicals that can be harmful to your animals and can do more harm than good with unwanted side effects. They are also more expensive, and it can take a while to see any real results. For this reason, you should consider natural options. Herbal remedies are a great alternative and much safer for your livestock.

This chapter explains herbal remedies and their historical use. It also presents some of the most common remedies with simple step-by-step instructions.

What Are Herbal Remedies?

Herbal remedies, also called botanical medicine, botanic therapy, and phytotherapy, are natural medicines made from different plant parts like stems, bark, flowers, roots, berries, and leaves. They are used to treat or prevent various diseases. Unlike regular medicines, herbal remedies aren't tested or regulated. Herbs are plants that are used for their savory, aromatic, and medicinal qualities.

Herbal remedies are among the most ancient treatments in the world.
https://pixabay.com/photos/natural-medicine-flower-essences-1738161/

Herbal remedies are among the most ancient treatments in the world. Most of the modern medicinal recipes are derived from folk medicine.

Historical Use of Herbal Medicine

People have used herbs and traditional livestock medicines for thousands of years. Herbs were extremely popular in many ancient cultures as they were used for different purposes. For instance, the Romans purified the air with dill.

One of the most renowned Greek physicians, Hippocrates, also found 400 herbs to treat diseases. Another Greek physician, Pedanius Dioscorides, wrote a book called "De Materia Medica" where he listed the benefits and medicinal uses of a variety of herbs. To this day, many people still use this book as a reference for natural medicine.

The ancient Egyptians also used plants as remedies. Archeologists found an ancient papyrus containing 700 medical formulas that were surprisingly advanced. They talked about using herbs like bayberry, basil, and aloe for medicinal purposes.

In the Middle Ages, people used herbs to preserve meat, cover rotten taste in food, and mask unpleasant body odors. Interestingly, herbal medicine wasn't popular at the time because it was associated with paganism and witchcraft. American Indians also knew about the significance of herbal remedies from their ancestors and grew different herbs in their gardens.

Herbalism reached its highest popularity from the 15th to the 17th centuries. Greek and Latin books were translated into English, and they were in high demand.

Throughout the years, herbalism faced many challenges with its association with witchcraft or others accusing it of being old wives' tales. However, things changed in the 20th century when the Council on Medical Education set standards for the medical use of herbs. However, many schools didn't put teaching herbs high on their list. Luckily, in the last 50 years, there has been a growing interest in folk medicine and herbalism, with many herbal remedies sold either online or in stores.

There isn't much evidence to show how people started using herbs as medicine or discovered which plants were safe for use and which were toxic. However, in 1 A.D., the Roman herbalist Pliny wrote that humans learned about safe herbs from animals like deer, dogs, and swallows.

Over the years, people have used herbs to cure their illnesses and treat their livestock and pets. Evidence from 60,000 years ago proves that humans used the same medicinal plants on themselves and their animals.

Herbs have been used to treat parasites in animals for centuries as well. Many ancient records showed people used extracts of garlic, castor oil, and areca nuts to control parasites in animals.

Growing Interest in Herbal Alternatives in Parasite Control

In the last few years, more and more people have been turning their attention to herbal remedies to treat their livestock. Natural medicine is better than traditional medicine in many respects. It doesn't cause many side effects, doesn't contain chemicals or artificial additives, is affordable, and doesn't cause irritation in the stomach.

Since you are raising livestock for meat and other products, you want to make sure these products are safe and clean. So, animals shouldn't contain any drug residue from medicines like anthelmintics or antibiotics, which can cause health problems to the people consuming their meat. Many farmers are treating their livestock with herbal remedies instead of chemical medicines to guarantee their livestock's safety and protect their family's health.

Are Herbal Remedies Effective?

Many people often wonder whether herbal remedies are effective on humans and animals. Well, if they weren't effective, would they still be popular worldwide after all these years?

In Asia and other countries, people use medicinal plants to treat parasites and worms in livestock. After using plants like Hedysarum coronarium and Lotus pedunculatus to treat their sheep, they noticed a 50% decrease in worm infestation. Tannin oil has also proved effective in weakening parasite activities in livestock.

According to a study published in Herald Scholarly Open Access, medicinal herbs with antibacterial activity, like turmeric, ginger, thyme, cinnamon, and cloves, can treat parasites in cattle.

In another study conducted by Cambridge University, many herbs with antiparasitic properties, like coconut oil, clove oil, anise, and goldthread, were shown to be effective in treating worms in farm animals.

Limitations of Herbal Remedies

Herbal remedies, like any type of medication, have their own limitations. Unfortunately, all the evidence that proves the effectiveness of herbal medicine is very limited. Although some scientific research backs them, their results and success are mainly based on traditional use.

A Cambridge University study also found that not all antiparasitic plants are effective. For instance, the neem tree effectively treats gastrointestinal diseases and other parasite-related issues in livestock. However, when its leaves were used to treat a sheep suffering from parasites, there was no anthelmintic effect.

A List of Herbal Remedies for Parasite Control

There are many types of medicinal plants in nature, and each has its own usage and benefits. This section explores herbal remedies with anthelmintic properties commonly used for parasite control. Anthelmintic plants kill intestinal parasites or eliminate them.

Aloe Vera

Although aloe vera is known for its soothing properties, it also has other benefits. The plant can eliminate or destroy parasites and protect the animals from further infections.

Active Ingredients:

- **Hormones:** They have anti-inflammatory properties and can heal wounds.
- **Fatty Acids:** They have anti-inflammatory properties.
- **Anthraquinones:** They have antiviral and antibacterial properties.
- **Sugars:** Provide the body with fructose and glucose.
- **Minerals** like zinc, sodium, potassium, manganese, magnesium, selenium, copper, chromium, and calcium.
- **Enzymes:** Reduce inflammation.
- **Vitamins** like choline, folic acid, and vitamins A, B12, C, and E.

Mechanisms of Action:

- **Antiseptic Effect:** Helps fight against viruses, bacteria, and fungi.
- **Antiviral Properties:** Boosts the immune system and protects it against infections.
- **Laxative Effects:** Increases mucus secretion and water connection in the intestines.
- **Anti-Inflammatory** properties.
- **Healing Properties:** Accelerates wound contraction.

Chamomile

Chamomile has anthelmintic properties and is high in tannin compounds. It paralyzes the parasite and reduces the egg-hatching process.

Active Compounds:

- Rutin
- Luteolin
- Apigenin
- Quercetin

These compounds have antioxidant and antibacterial properties.

Mechanisms of Action:

- Anti-cancer properties
- Anti-inflammatory properties
- Protects against cardiovascular issues
- Treats diarrhea

- Treats eczema
- Treats gastrointestinal conditions
- Boosts immune system

Coriander

Coriander seeds are well known for their healing properties. They are considered as fungicidal, bactericidal, and larvicidal. They can eliminate parasites and protect your body from these microorganisms.

Active Compounds:

- Linalool
- Terpinene
- Pinene
- Camphor
- Limonene
- Geranyl acetate
- Cymene
- Bornyl acetate
- Thymol
- Gallic acid

Mechanisms of Action:

- Anti-inflammatory properties
- Anti-cancer properties
- Relieves gastrointestinal discomfort
- Stimulates the liver to increase bile secretion

Garlic

Garlic is known for its antibacterial properties that can kill parasites in the gastrointestinal tract. It also has other health benefits, like improving the animals' immune systems and protecting them from new parasite infestations.

Garlic is known for its antibacterial properties that can kill parasites in the gastrointestinal tract.
https://pixabay.com/photos/garlic-ingredient-flavoring-3419544/

Active Compounds:

- **Organosulfur Compounds:** allicin, ajoene, alliin, allyl propyl disulfide, diallyl polysulfides, vinyl thins, diallyl tetrasulfide, diallyl sulfide, diallyl disulfide, diallyl trisulfide, and allyl methyl trisulfide.

- **Phenolic Compounds:** like sinapic acids, coumaric, hydroxybenzoic, vanillin ferulic, and caffeic.

- **Saponins:** like eruboside B and proto-eruboside B.

These compounds have antibacterial and antioxidant properties.

Mechanisms of Action:

- Antimicrobial properties
- Stimulates the immune system
- Protects against cardiovascular issues
- Anti-cancer properties
- Protects the digestive system

Ginger

Ginger is one of the most popular herbal remedies, and people have been using it for centuries to treat the digestive system. Although there isn't enough evidence to support its effect on parasites in livestock, there is no harm in experimenting with it. Add it to your animals' food every week and observe the results.

Active Compounds:

- Terpene compounds
- Phenolic, like paradols, shogaols, and gingerols
- Polyphenols like 10-gingerol and 8-gingerol

Mechanism of Action:

- Antimicrobial properties
- Antitumor properties
- Anti-inflammatory properties

Neem

People who used chemical remedies found neem a great and effective alternative. It doesn't only eliminate parasites but also protects livestock from fungal diseases. To protect their animals against parasites, farmers feed their livestock neem cake in some parts of India and use the plant's oils and leaves to prevent parasitic infections.

Active Compounds:

- Azadirachtin
- Quercetin
- Salannin
- Gedunin
- Sodium nimbinate
- Nimbidol
- Nimbidin
- Nimbin

Mechanisms of Action:

- Anti-inflammatory properties
- Anti-cancer properties
- Antioxidants properties

Pot Marigold

Pot marigold has antimicrobial properties and can be an effective treatment against any diseases caused by parasites or any other microorganisms.

Active Compounds:
- Lutein
- Sesquiterpene glycosides
- Saponins
- Triterpene glycosides
- Oleanane-type
- Triterpene oligoglycosides
- Flavonol glycoside

Mechanisms of Action:
- Antifungal properties
- Reduces inflammation
- Antioxidant properties

Pumpkin Seeds

Pumpkin seeds can be an effective treatment against tapeworms and other types of intestinal parasites. These seeds are high in amino acid cucurbits and can paralyze the parasites and expel them from the gastrointestinal tract.

Active Compounds:
- Cucurbitacins
- Tocopherols
- Phenolic compounds
- Unsaturated fatty acids
- Phytosterols
- Amino acids

Mechanisms of Action:
- Contains Omega-3 and omega-6 fatty acids
- Antioxidants properties
- Eliminates and protects from parasites

Tannin-Rich Plants

Tannin is a compound that can reduce or remove parasites in the digestive tract. Many herbs contain tannins, like sage, coriander, rosemary, mint, and licorice.

Active Compounds:
- Gallic acids
- D-glucose

Mechanisms of Action:
- Anti-inflammatory properties
- Healing wounds
- Antioxidant properties

Turmeric

Curcumin is one of the substances found in turmeric and has antiparasitic properties. It can also eliminate adult worms.

Active Compounds:
- Curcumin
- Volatile oil
- Curcuminoids

Mechanisms of Action:
- Anti-inflammatory properties
- Anti-cancer properties
- Antimicrobial properties

Wormwood

People have been using wormwood for centuries to kill human and animal parasites. They also strengthen the body's immune system and protect it against worms. This herb is extremely safe and has no side effects.

Active Compounds:
- Thujone
- Coumarins
- Flavonoids
- Phenolic acids
- Artemisinin
- Absinthin isomers

Mechanisms of Action:
- Aids in digestion
- Antifungal and antibacterial properties

- Protects the liver
- Anti-inflammatory properties
- Boosts the immune system
- Antioxidants properties
- Protect nerve cells
- Relieves pain

Making and Administering Herbal Remedies

Now that you understand the significance of herbal remedies, you are ready to discover various natural medicine formulations to treat your livestock.

Tea

Instructions:

1. Pick the leaves and roots of any of the plants mentioned here.
2. Leave them to dry in a warm and dark place.
3. After they dry, store them in labeled jars in a cool, dark place.
4. Take 1 teaspoon of dry leaves or roots and brew tea by adding hot water to them.

Strong Tea Brew

Instructions:

1. Simmer one teaspoon of plant parts in a stainless steel teapot.
2. Leave it to cool down, but don't remove the lid.
3. Use it while it is still fresh.

Put the tea in a syringe and administer it into the animals' mouths. You can give them this remedy once a day for a week. Make sure it's cooled down before they consume it.

Tincture #1

Instructions:

1. Cut or dice the plants' leaves or roots in a glass jar.
2. Pour in alcohol like vodka to cover the plant's parts, or mix the alcohol with water.
3. Cover the jar with a lid, label it, and add the date.
4. Store it for six weeks in a cool and dark place.

You can remove the plant material if you prefer and only store the liquid. If you don't want to use alcohol, use vinegar or glycerine instead. However, if you plan to store it for a long period of time, adding alcohol is the better option since it has a long shelf life.

Put the tincture in a dropper bottle and give your animal 10 to 15 drops once a day for a week.

Tincture #2

Ingredients:

- 1 1/4 cups of glycerin
- 2 smashed garlic cloves
- 1 tablespoon of oregano
- 1 tablespoon of thyme
- 1 tablespoon of Oregon grape root

2 tablespoons of echinacea leaves or roots **Instructions:**

1. Mix all the ingredients minus the glycerin.
2. Add the glycerin.
3. Put the mixture in a glass jar and seal it tightly.
4. Store the jar in a cool and dark place for a month.
5. Shake the jar once every day.
6. After one month, pour the tincture into a glass dropper bottle.

Administer by mouth by putting 10 to 15 drops in the animal's mouth or water.

Paste

Ingredients:

- 1 tablespoon of beeswax
- 1 tablespoon of dry herbs

2 tablespoons of olive oil **Instructions:**

1. Fill a jar with dry herbs, then pour the olive oil.
2. Put the jar in a dry and warm place and cover it with a cheesecloth to protect it from insects and dust.
3. Store it for six weeks to let the oil infuse.
4. Check the jar regularly for mold.
5. After the oil is infused, add the beeswax to create a paste.

Apply on your animal when needed.

Tonic

Ingredients:

- 2 cups of wormwood
- 2 cups of thyme leaf
- 2 cups of sage leaf
- 1 cup of rosemary leaf powder
- 1 cup of psyllium seed powder
- 1 cup of mustard seed powder
- 1 cup of ginger root powder
- 1 cup of garlic powder
- 1 cup of cayenne pepper powder
- 1 cup of black walnut hull powder
- 1 cup of anise seed powder (optional)
- 1/2 cup of powdered cloves
- 1 cup of cinnamon powder
- 2 cups of diatomaceous earth (Although it is a very effective remedy against parasites, it can make the tonic feel dusty, which can be hard on your animals' lungs. You can feed it to your animal separately to speed the healing process.)

Instructions:

1. Mix all the ingredients, then place them in a glass jar and label it.
2. Store in a cool and dark place.
3. Administer for a week, twice daily, and every six to eight weeks, or as needed.

N.B. Don't use black walnut or wormwood if your animal is pregnant. Equines should never consume black walnuts.

Herbal Dosage Ball

Ingredients:

- 1/2 cup of powdered herb
- 1/4 cup of flour (to hold the mixture together)
- 1/4 cup of honey or molasses

Instructions:

1. Mix the first two ingredients, then add the honey or molasses.
2. Knead them into a dough with your fingers or in a food processor.
3. Break it into 12 small balls, then coat each with the flour.

Only feed your animal one ball a day. You can feed it to them by hand, and they might eat it right away. If they don't, shove it into their mouth. In most cases, they will like it and swallow it. However, they might not and spit it out. If this happens, shove it further back. Break the ball into pieces for baby animals.

You can feed it to them by hand, and they might eat it right away.

Salves
Ingredients:

- 1 tablespoon of honey
- 1 tablespoon of beeswax
- 2 tablespoons of calendula-infused oil
- 2 tablespoons of oregano-infused oil
- 2 tablespoons of chamomile-infused oi.

Instructions:

1. Melt the beeswax and oils in a double boiler.
2. Then, pour them into a jar and leave them to cool down.
3. Once they cool down, add the honey to the jar.
4. Seal it tightly with a lid, and you can use it for 6 to 12 months.

Apply on your animal's infected area twice a day until they heal.

Bath Soap

Ingredients:

- 2 drops of eucalyptus essential oil
- 2 drops of tea tree essential oil
- 3 drops of oregano essential oil
- 3 drops of lavender essential oil

3 cups of Castille soap **Instructions**:

1. Mix all the ingredients and place them in a glass bottle.
2. Shower the animal with the soap once every two months.
3. Scrub and lather your animal well.

N.B. Some dosages may differ depending on the size and number of animals, so consult your vet to be safe.

Safety Concerns

Although herbal remedies are effective and beneficial, there are a few safety concerns you should be aware of to guarantee your livestock's safety.

Potential Toxicity

Not all herbs are safe, and some are extremely toxic for cattle. You should be aware of toxic herbs and avoid them to keep your livestock and family safe.

Water Hemlock

This is one of the most toxic and dangerous plants in North America. If your animal consumes a small amount, they can get very sick or even die.

Signs of Water Hemlock Poisoning:

- Excessive drooling
- Nervousness

- Fast heartbeat
- Muscle twitching
- Pupils dilation
- Rapid breathing
- Tremors
- Seizures
- Coma
- Death

Lupine

If a pregnant cow consumes lupine, her babies will most likely be crooked, possibly having skeletal defects or a cleft palate.

Signs of Lupine Poisoning:

- Depression
- Nervousness
- Convulsions
- Lack of muscle control
- Trouble breathing
- Lethargy
- Coma
- Death

Death Camas

Judging from the name, consuming this plant can be fatal for your livestock. So make sure to keep your animals away from it.

Signs of Death Camas Poisoning:

- Trouble breathing
- Nausea
- Vomiting
- Weak muscles
- Heart failure
- Lung congestion
- Coma
- Death

Poison Hemlock

Poison hemlock can also cause birth defects in piglets and calves.

Signs of Poison Hemlock Poisoning:

- Weak pulse
- Trembling
- Paralysis
- Depression
- Pupils dilation
- Convulsion
- Respiratory paralysis
- Bloody feces
- Coma
- Death

Nightshades

Nightshade can be toxic to poultry, sheep, swine, cattle, and horses.

Signs of Nightshades Poisoning:

- Trouble breathing with expiratory grunt
- Drowsiness
- Trembling
- Paralysis
- Progressive weakening
- Nasal discharge
- High temperature
- Skin turning yellow
- Distended gallbladder

Black Cherry

Signs of Black Cherry Poisoning:

- Trouble breathing
- Staggering
- Convulsion
- Anxiety
- Collapse

• Sudden death

Tips to Safely Use Herbal Medicine

It is better to be safe than sorry. Using natural medicine is tricky. One mistake can risk your animals' lives. Follow these tips so you can safely use herbal remedies.

- Learn about poisonous herbs and keep them away from your animals.
- When you are preparing a remedy at home, follow the instructions and the recommended dosage.
- If you buy herbal medicine from a store, check the ingredients, expiration date, side effects, and dosage before using.
- Only buy your herbs from a licensed herbalist.
- Learn everything about herbs, and don't hesitate to ask your vet if you have any concerns.
- Call the vet immediately if you give your animal herbal medicine, and they start showing any side effects.
- Watch out for allergic reactions. Call your vet if your animal has trouble breathing after you give him the medicine.
- If your animals take other medications, consult your vet before giving them herbal remedies.

Challenges with Using Herbal Remedies

Many people have encountered some challenges when using herbal remedies. For instance, some people used any type of herb, believing they were all the same. Naturally, they didn't see any real results. After some research, they realized there are specific herbs for treating parasites and started using them. Some livestock owners also didn't pay attention to the dosage guidelines and gave their animals high dosages, making them sick. After consulting their vets, they realized their mistake.

Some farmers found that their animals were getting sicker after the medicine. However, they later discovered that it was the medication's side effect. Some realized their mistake after losing their animals. Since then, they would always observe their animals after giving them medication to see if something was wrong.

You can't predict how your animal will react to an herbal remedy. They might get an allergy reaction, start showing side effects, or start getting better. Don't walk away from them after you give them the medication. Stay close for 20 to 30 minutes to observe their reaction. If everything seems fine and they aren't reacting strangely towards the remedy, then continue with the medication.

You and your family's safety depends on the health of your livestock. Consider treating them with natural remedies and stay away from harmful chemicals. Herbal medicine has existed since the beginning of time, and its popularity hasn't slowed down for a reason. It is effective and safe. However, if your animal isn't improving, you should consider traditional medicine. In some cases, it might be your only option.

Chapter 7: Additional Natural Strategies

Besides all the natural methods discussed in the previous chapters, there are additional natural approaches for holistic parasite management since integrating more than one measure is essential to achieve sustainable control of the parasites. This chapter explores these alternative strategies, based on scientific research and case studies, illustrating the successful application of those strategies in different livestock production systems.

Using Diatomaceous Earth

Due to a more than generous application of antiparasitic drugs in the past, parasites becoming resistant to artificial anthelmintics has become a growing concern for livestock owners. Diatomaceous earth (DE) can be a suitable alternative treatment for internal parasites because it doesn't lead to antiparasitic resistance. In goats and other ruminants, there is also the problem of weak innate and acquired immunity to ringworm infections, which can't be solved with other natural methods. Also known as Diatomite, diatomaceous earth, on the other hand, has been used for deworming livestock and other animals and even expelling GIT parasites from people's intestines for centuries. Besides being a dewormer, diatomaceous earth can also be used for insecticidal treatment, a filtering agent for air and water, supplements, and food additives. The minerals in this compound can also boost nutrition and growth in farm animals, leading to higher live weight gains and improved heat tolerance (particularly beneficial in sheep). Moreover, while it's primarily used for controlling internal parasites, it can also be effective against external ones like lice and fleas.

What Is Diatomaceous Earth?

Diatomaceous earth is a powder made from naturally occurring sedimentary rocks that are the remnants of fossilized algae.
SprocketRocket, CC0, via Wikimedia Commons:
https://commons.wikimedia.org/wiki/File:Diatomaceous_Earth.jpg

Diatomaceous earth is a powder made from naturally occurring sedimentary rocks that are the remnants of fossilized algae. A small quantity of diatomaceous earth powder contains millions of Diatoms, microscopic hard-shell algae that populated the earth millions of years ago. Deposited in seas and lakes, the shells turned into sediments, and when these water sources dried out, the result was a silicon-rich compound. Besides silicone, diatomaceous earth also contains other minerals in varying amounts, depending on its source.

How Does Diatomaceous Earth Work?

Several theories support how diatomaceous earth can help control and eliminate parasites from inside and outside the host's body. According to one, the effectiveness of this compound against intestinal parasites can be seen in the shape of the particles. They look like a cylinder riddled with holes and have a negative charge. As all those tiny cylinders move through the body, their negative charge attracts everything with a positive charge, which, besides heavy metals, also applies to the outer layer of many intestinal parasites and pathogens. The holes absorb everything the cylinders attract, trapping them inside the particles. Once trapped, the host has no problem eliminating them through the intestinal system. The good bacteria in the gastrointestinal tract have a neutral or negative charge, so they won't be affected by the particles – one of the major benefits of using diatomaceous earth. Moreover, eliminating the parasites from the digestive tract helps keep a healthy balance in the microbiome of good bacteria, improving the hosts' appetite and contributing to better weight gain. A healthy gut microbiome will also boost their immunity, rendering them less vulnerable to future infections and parasite infestations.

Another way diatomaceous earth acts against gastrointestinal parasites, specifically worms, is by breaking their life cycle. For example, several studies (Laing et al. 2013, Beltran and Martin 2015, Islam et al. 2016) showed that regular treatment with diatomaceous earth can prevent roundworm larvae from migrating from the dung to the herbage, where ruminants would consume it. Interrupting the parasite's life cycle this way ensures that the number of parasites on the pastures reduces over time, ultimately reducing the number of parasites carried by the host.

A similar theory correlates diatomaceous earth particles' small, sharp edges with their abrasive action on a coating of cysts and external parasitic insects. The particles scratch the waterproof surface of these animals' external coating and absorb lipids from their exoskeleton, eventually causing them to die. Whereas, yet another theory (Köster, 2010) claims that due to its unique composition, diatomaceous earth works together with digestive enzymes, acting as a buffer to create a hostile environment for gastrointestinal parasites, preventing them from feeding and reproducing.

According to a study searching for a less invasive alternative for worm control in pigeons (M. WIEWIÓRA et al., 2015), regularly giving the birds diatomaceous earth supplements significantly diminishes the number of parasites in the digestive tract. Scientists have confirmed the effectiveness of this approach on livestock, pets, and even people, which is why you can buy diatomaceous earth in different formulations (food-grade for humans, for various types of animals, etc.)

Benefits notwithstanding, some studies (Rahmann, G., & Seip, H., n.d.) show that while diatomaceous earth might affect parasite loads measured by fecal egg counts, it does not reduce some serious symptoms caused by internal and vector-borne parasites (for example, they found that anemia often remains even after the parasites have been expelled).

When using it for livestock parasite control, diatomaceous earth can be applied internally and externally. For example, if the animals are infested with fleas, powder specifically formulated for this purpose can be applied to their skin or fur. They must be dusted daily until the fleas die off and the animal's skin clears up. The treatment must be applied to all animals in the same group/location, regardless of whether they are affected. The fleas can migrate and hide within the fur of new hosts, so treating all animals is always recommended.

To apply diatomaceous earth against internal parasites, the powder should be dissolved in water and given to animals regularly (following the manufacturer's instructions). The process involves giving the supplement to the animals for several days until the amount of worms and eggs expelled through feces is reduced to the minimum acceptable limit. Use regular measurements and consult guides for acceptable minimums for different animals to combat parasitic infections and prevent their return.

Using Forage Plants and Trees with Bioactive Compounds

Plant material from foraged plants and trees contains natural bioactive compounds that deter or eliminate parasites from the host's body, making them an excellent resource for eliminating parasitic infections in animal husbandry. For example, the Nordic countries have a long and well-established history of using plants as natural anthelmintics for both animals and humans – and for a good reason.

How Can Plants Help Combat Parasitic Infestations?

Besides being nutrient-dense and helping meet animals' nutrient needs, plants are also packed with antiparasitic compounds called nutraceuticals. These are metabolites and secondary plant substances (compared to the compounds they are mainly used for and which provide nutritional value), like tannins, potent antiparasitic agents. Many plants contain tannins, but only those with high condensed tannins levels are suitable for controlling and combating parasitic infestations. These tannin-rich plants are known as bioactive forage but also have another benefit. Unlike plants used for medicinal purposes, which often have side effects and consequently have to be used carefully and with due precaution, tanniferous plants are non-toxic. If necessary, they can be applied in larger doses and across a long period. They can even be incorporated into the normal diet of livestock as a supplement to other plant materials used for feeding.

There are several theories on how condensed tannins help combat livestock parasites. According to a popular one, when they come in contact with the surface of the parasite's body, these compounds create a powerful reaction hindering the parasite's metabolic functions, food intake, reproduction, and mobility. According to another theory, tannin-rich bioforge also has an indirect way of acting against parasites. Supporters of this theory argue that when ingested, condensed tannins bind proteins to themselves, forming complexes that can withstand digestive degradation (particularly strong in ruminants). This way, proteins can get through the digestive tract, where they'll be absorbed. Some parasites, like nematodes, cause protein degradation and loss in the intestines, preventing the host from taking this essential nutrient. Because proteins are the building blocks of cells and essential for many metabolic processes, reduced protein intake results in impaired metabolic functions, one of which is immunity. By helping get more protein to the intestines, condensed tannins can balance protein levels and provide the host with much-needed resources for boosting their immunity and resilience to parasites and other intruders.

How to Use Tanniferous Plants

There are several options for integrating tanniferous plants into livestock diets. For example, they can be cultivated as arable crops and used in the normal feeding rotation as a preventive measure before an expected infestation. Or, they can be preserved as silage or hay and used, for example, for deworming later when infestation occurs. However, some studies suggest that using tanniferous plants this way might have negative consequences, too, including reduced feed intake or feed digestibility (Dawson et al., 1999), if the proper measures aren't followed. For example, not all tanniferous plants will provide enough nutrition or be suitable for digestion for all livestock types. According to another study (Coop and Kyriazakis, 2001), in small ruminants, these negative consequences are often outweighed by the positive impact of a parasite-free herd on productivity and economic gain.

Which Plants to Use for Parasite Control

Phytotherapy is a science-based prophylactic or therapeutic application of plants or bioactive compounds gained from plants for preventing or curing diseases. According to a study, this approach can be divided into traditional and allopathic phytotherapy (Hördegen, 2005). The former is based on generations of practices passed down through oral traditions (some of which are still used today and proven effective by modern science). The allopathic approach relies on scientific verification of anthelmintic plants or their bioactive components. This verification also considers possible risks and side effects, as is the case with the following description of plants with anthelmintic effects backed by science.

Trees and Shrubs

Trees and shrubs are particularly commonly used as a treatment against parasites. For example, Willow (Salix spp) has proven anthelmintic effects and anti-inflammatory actions, which are additional benefits when combating parasitic infections. Feeding willow leaves to livestock eliminates the worms and larvae from their body, while the bark can be effective against flukes. A decoction can be created from the bark and added to the animal's water to get the maximum benefits.

In some areas, their widespread availability is a vast reason shrubs and trees are the most viable solution for natural antiparasitic measures. For example, small ruminants like sheep often graze on a broad range of herbage (including trees and shrubs), so they'll likely take to beneficial ones, too. Increasing the variety of plants they can graze on is proven to be correlated with the sheep's improved resilience to parasitic nematodes (Diaz Lira et al., 2005).

Herbaceous Plants

A wide variety of herbaceous plants have been used against parasitic infections and have proven effective in reducing the harmful effects of parasite infestation in livestock. One of the most widely used natural anthelmintics is derived from the plant called goosefoot or American wormseed (chenopodium ambrosioides). Archeological records suggest that the oil derived from this plant has been used for several centuries. For example, in the 18th century, Swedish botanist Peter Kalm noted when visiting North America that European settlers in the American colonies and the indigenous inhabitants used chenopodium extract for treating ascaris (nematode) infections. It has since been proven that the principal ingredient in this plant is ascaridole, a terpene found in many other herbaceous plants, too – which are now cultivated as crops for grazing or to be preserved for later anthelmintic supplementation. Many herbs used as herbs have antiparasitic effects. Studies (Eminov, 1982.) found that many of these plants are effective against trichostrongylus larvae in sheep.

According to ancient Roman literature, plants of the Asteraceae family have also been used to treat parasitic infections. The Romans used dried, not-yet-opened flowers of Artemisia species to expel ascaris and tapeworms from animals and people. The active ingredient in these plants is santonin, which modern veterinary and pharmacological studies have widely researched. For example, researchers found that santonin has a neurotoxic effect on worms in low quantities, specifically targeting the ganglia of their nerve rings (Saunders Company, 1957). The common tansy (Tanacetum vulgare) is also a member of the Asteraceae family. Known for its active component, thujone, this plant is a widely used deworming agent in the Northern Hemisphere.

Other plants with widespread use against parasites are berries and common vegetables belonging to the onion family (allium spp.), the cabbage family (brassica spp.), and even carrots (Daucus carota). Likewise, in tropical regions, cucumber and pumpkin seeds are traditionally used for expelling tapeworms and larvae from the host's intestines. When the practice spread to other parts of the world, scientists proved that these plants contain cucurbitin, a potent antiparasitic agent. It's still considered one of the safest antiparasitic measures in non-ruminants across the world.

Besides its widespread use for smoking, the tobacco plant was also used for treating nematode infestations in tropical regions. Tobacco infusions were a common practice for keeping parasites away from ruminant livestock until the appearance of synthetic anthelmintics.

Pasture Plants

Probably the most effective way of incorporating plants to control parasitic infections is by using specialized crops for grazing. Due to this, this approach has attracted much attention and is currently the focus of researchers worldwide. So far, the most condensed tannins among pasture plants were found in legumes. For example, lotus major (lotus pedunculatus) is packed with proanthocyanidins, which is associated with reduced worm infestation in grazing lambs (Niezen JH et al., 1985).

Quebracho has a similarly powerful anthelmintic effect and can kill adult nematodes and their larvae in several types of livestock.

Lichens and Ferns

One of the plants most commonly used in the traditional Nordic antiparasitic measure approaches is a fern called Dryopteris filix-mas. Moreover, the ancient Greeks also used this plant (specifically, a powder made from its rhizome) against tapeworms. Like this fern, other lichens and ferns also contain silicic acid, which acts as a potent anthelmintic agent.

Plant Compounds

Besides using whole plants or plant parts like leaves, seeds, etc., you can also use compounds containing active ingredients for treating parasitic infections. For example, garlic powder is an excellent dewormer and can be used as a livestock supplement. Similarly, you find ground-up mustard, fennel, carrot seeds, wild ginger, goosefoot, and pyrethrum in powder or oil form. Pyrethrum (made from chrysanthemum flower) is the most effective in powder form. Neem oil is a powerful insecticide extracted from the Indian neem tree and is another excellent alternative for ectoparasites.

To apply it externally and eliminate ectoparasites, regularly run the powder or oil along the animal's infested areas until the parasites are gone. Internal application should be based on the manufacturer's recommendations for each compound.

Another study (Rahmann, G., & Seip, H., n.d.) found the following plants to be effective in curing and controlling endo-parasite diseases in livestock:

- Chicory (cichorium intybus)
- Birdsfoot Trefoil (lotus corniculatus and lotus pedunculatus)
- Sulla (hedysarum coronarium)
- Sainfoin (onobrychis viciifolia)
- Quebracho (schinopsis spp.)
- Socarillo (dorycnium pentaphyllum)
- Chinese Lespedeza (lespedeza cuneata)
- Dock (rumex obtusifolius)
- Wattle leaves (acacia karroo)
- Heather (calluna vulgaris)

- Chestnut Tree (fruit – Castanea sativa)
- Common Dogwood (cornus sanguinea)
- Hazel tree (Corylus avellana)
- Erica (erica ssp)
- Pine tree (leaves – pinus sylvestris)
- Pomegranate (Punica granatum)
- Oak (Quercus spp)
- Black Locust (robinia pseudo acacia)
- Blackberry bush (rubus fruticosus)
- Willow (salix spp)
- Genista (leaves – sarothamnus scoparius)
- Grape Seed (extract – Vitis spp)

Selective Breeding Programs

Selective breeding programs rely on animals' inherent capacity to resist diseases they were previously not exposed to. As hosts, these animals can obstruct and alter the parasite's life cycle and become resistant to the illnesses the parasites carry or cause. Natural resistance is genetically coded, which means that by breeding resistant specimens, one can increase the resistance level in the next generation. Incorporating this genetic element into parasite and disease control in animal husbandry has many benefits. It creates a permanent change in the animal's genetic material, ensuring the consistency of the resistance and removing the need for further measures – which isn't the case with other natural parasite control methods that must be repeated or supplemented regularly. Moreover, through selective breeding, resistance to several diseases can be increased simultaneously.

Selective breeding can take many forms, depending on the available resources and the type of parasites. Some of the most popular techniques for achieving this goal include selecting specimens with the highest resistance levels for specific parasites and diseases, choosing the appropriate breeds based on the environment, and using crossbreeding to introduce genes into well-adapted species depending on the desired outcomes.

The method known as "marker-assisted selection," which involves identifying the biochemical, morphological, and genetic (DNA or RNA) markers connected to the degree of disease resistance, is frequently used to choose breeds and individual specimens. Since these markers are genetically associated with the characteristic, they serve as a trustworthy means of selecting the right animals for selective breeding. Screenable markers are linked to easily identifiable genotypes, while selectable markers are more suited for removing particular, typically undesired, genotypes. Since DNA may be reproduced in vitro and utilized as much as possible, marker-assisted selection offers a cost-effective method of selective breeding since it allows for assessing many markers with a single purified sample. This lowers the price of marking and selects breeds appropriate for the procedure.

Single nucleotide polymorphism detection is one technique that can be used to identify genetic markers. Molecular codes known as linked markers are found in close proximity to genes that encode resistance. For instance, ruminants have a number of phenotypic (physical) and genetic markers known to be encoded in genes located close to those that determine immunity to gastrointestinal parasites. Another option is to use the major histocompatibility complex (MHC), which contains many polymorphic genes that determine how animals react immunologically to infections and parasites. Two of the three MHC classes are linked to resistance in ruminants and belong to class 2.

Defining what traits to measure regarding resistance is another crucial question. One of the most popular ones is Fecal Egg Count (FEC), which is heritable – although its heritability varies depending on the animal breed and parasite species. Immune response evaluation is another useful trait to use for these purposes.

According to a study investigating the effects of genetic manipulation by selective breeding for improving resistance to gastrointestinal nematodes in sheep (Windon, R. G. 1990), this approach can be a reliable alternative for chemical parasitic control. This study relied on the genetic variation linked to nematode resistance in sheep, along with previous experiments proving the feasibility of creating breeds with a higher resistance level. The conductors of the study also considered immunity, seeing it as a major cause of host animals' resistance to parasites. Based on this, they also concluded that for selective breeding to act as a control measure against parasitic infestation, several things must happen:

- A reasonable heritability level must exist for the selected marker to maximize the response to selection.
- The method must be cost-effective when compared to other natural and artificial measures.
- Ideally, the found resistance should be non-specific – in other words, it acts against several different parasites.
- The selection must be based on a linked trait that doesn't require contact with the parasite to identify resistance.
- The process should not adversely affect livestock production in the next generation.
- The selection should ensure that if parasite adaptation occurs to the host's resistance, it will remain manageable with other measures.

While selective breeding can provide the advantage of using breed-inclusive variation for improving resistance to parasites, selection based on this criterion alone can have negative effects. For example, some breeds or individuals used for selective breeding might have high resistance but a low live weight gain. Along with the benefits of parasite control, the latter will also be emphasized in the next generation, leading to economic losses. Although selective breeding can eliminate other natural control procedures like pasture management, it can be used within an integrated approach to limit production losses and minimize costs.

Using Copper

Copper sulfate and copper oxide are naturally occurring substances often used as an antiparasitic measure. When ruminants ingest copper sulfate, it remains in their rumen, releasing trace particles of copper. These trace mineral particles interject into the parasite-host relationships, disrupting it and creating a hostile environment for the parasite. Studies (Bang et al., 1990) found that regular administration of copper compounds leads to a reasonable reduction of parasite number for some parasite species. Based on another study (Burke et al., 2004), the optimal dosage of copper compounds for expelling parasitic worms from lambs without causing toxicity is 0.07 ounces per dose. Mixing it with animal feed or drinking water is the easiest application of copper sulfate or copper oxide. It's recommended to follow the manufacturer's recommendation for the specific copper sulfate compound you're using.

Chapter 8: Livestock Parasites and Climate Change

Long-term changes in climatic conditions, precipitation, and temperature are brought about by climate change, which is also changing Earth's average weather patterns. This issue is mostly caused by greenhouse gases like carbon dioxide (CO_2), methane (CH_4), and nitrous oxide (N_2O) that are unnecessarily released into the atmosphere as a result of human activity. The term "global warming" refers to the steady rise in global temperatures brought on by these gases' ability to retain solar heat.

The global impacts of climate change extend far beyond just temperature fluctuations and are deeply intertwined with the dynamics of livestock parasites. Here's a closer look at the critical global effects of climate change and how they are connected to livestock parasites:

Rising Temperatures

This warming environment influences the distribution and survival of a range of livestock parasites.

As global temperatures rise, so does the ambient temperature in many regions. This warming environment influences the distribution and survival of a range of livestock parasites. For example, some parasites that previously couldn't thrive in cooler areas may now find these regions more suitable, potentially exposing livestock to new parasitic threats.

Changing Precipitation Patterns

Traditional precipitation patterns change during climatic changes, leading to more frequent droughts and increased rainfall in some areas. These shifts in moisture availability affect the survival and propagation of parasites. For example, moisture-dependent parasites may thrive in regions experiencing more rainfall, while droughts diminish the availability of water sources needed for parasite development. During heavy rainfall and flooding, the dispersal of vector-borne parasites through mosquitoes and insects increases exponentially.

Biodiversity and Ecosystem Alterations

Changes in the climate disrupt the ecosystem, changing the distribution of wildlife and their parasites. As these changes occur, livestock may be exposed to new parasite vectors or reservoir hosts. Understanding these changes and gathering relevant information is crucial for effective parasite management.

Food and Water Resources

Changes in climate patterns bring changes to water and food availability for livestock. For example, in times of drought, water becomes scarce, and food supplies are limited, which can weaken the immune system, making livestock susceptible to parasitic infections. Likewise, extremely humid areas with persistent rainfall directly promote parasite dispersal.

Health Risks

Higher temperatures associated with climate change can influence the activity and distribution of disease vectors, which carry parasites and transmit diseases to humans and livestock. For instance, regions feasible for expansion of disease-carrying insects increase the risk of vector-borne parasites affecting livestock.

Economic and Livelihood Consequences

Climate change also leads to economic losses in the livestock industry due to reduced productivity, higher management costs for parasite control, and increased veterinary expenses. These economic consequences have a cascading impact on the livelihoods of individuals and communities dependent on livestock for income and sustenance.

Migration and Conflict

As climate change renders certain regions less habitable, it leads to population displacement, including livestock. Displaced livestock could carry parasites to new areas, potentially introducing novel parasitic challenges.

Although these challenges can become a nuisance when not dealt with properly, most factors that potentially increase the incidence of parasitic infections in livestock can be avoided by implementing strict quarantine and monitoring protocols.

The global impacts of climate change are intricately linked with the dynamics of livestock parasites. Temperature, precipitation, and extreme weather events influence the prevalence and distribution of these parasites. As explained earlier, addressing the health and productivity of livestock in a changing climate requires a comprehensive understanding of these interconnections and implementing adaptive and mitigative strategies for effective parasite management.

Parasite Life-Cycle Influences

As you already know, temperature, humidity, and precipitation affect the survival, development, and transmission of parasites, ultimately impacting the health and productivity of livestock. Here's how these factors can influence the life cycles of different parasites.

Temperature

Warmer temperatures accelerate the development of many parasites. For example, gastrointestinal nematodes like haemonchus contortus in sheep and cattle thrive in warm and humid conditions. These nematodes can quickly complete their life cycles in warm climates, leading to more frequent infections.

On the flip side, cold temperatures can slow down or halt the development of some parasites. Liver flukes (Fasciola hepatica), which infect the liver of cattle and sheep, are less active in cold conditions. As a result, their transmission is reduced in colder climates.

Humidity

High humidity creates favorable conditions for the survival of many external parasites. The poultry red mite (dermanyssus gallinae) is a blood-feeding ectoparasite that infects chickens. As high humidity is essential for the mite's survival, it leads to infestations in poultry houses, causing stress and reduced egg production.

On the other hand, low humidity can desiccate and kill certain parasites. For example, the eggs and larvae of some gastrointestinal nematodes are susceptible to desiccation. In arid regions with low humidity, limited transmission of these parasites is reported, further confirming the effects of humidity on parasites.

Precipitation

Increased rainfall creates breeding sites for parasites and their vectors. The stable fly (stomoxys calcitrans), which feeds on the blood of cattle, loves wet, decaying organic matter to breed in. Conversely, drought can reduce the availability of water sources, affecting livestock drinking behavior and potentially increasing the risk of waterborne parasites. For example, liver flukes require a freshwater snail as an intermediate host. In drought conditions, these freshwater snails fail to survive, disrupting the fluke's life cycle and limiting the chances of developing waterborne parasitic infections.

Specific parasite control measures you can take include adjusting deworming schedules, implementing vector control measures, and providing appropriate shelter and management practices to mitigate the impact of environmental factors on parasite transmission and livestock health.

Temperature-Dependent Parasites

Although mentioned earlier, it's an evident change that influences parasite distribution. Warmer temperatures associated with climate change enable the movement of temperature-sensitive parasites to higher altitudes and latitudes. For example, parasites previously limited to lower elevations may now find the climate suitable for survival and reproduction at higher altitudes.

- The liver fluke Fasciola hepatica, which primarily affected lowland areas, has been reported in higher altitudes and latitudes as temperatures have increased.
- The spread of ticks carrying Lyme disease (Ixodes scapularis) to more northern regions in North America as temperatures have risen.

Altered Ecosystems and Host Distribution

Human activity, habitat loss, and land use change can alter ecosystems, impacting parasite distribution. The loss of natural habitats disrupts ecological balances, leading to modification in host populations and consequently affecting parasites.

- Deforestation increases contact between humans and wildlife, potentially transmitting zoonotic parasites from wildlife to humans.
- Changes in agricultural practices may result in shifts in livestock populations, which can influence the distribution of livestock parasites.

Invasive Species and Trade

The global movement of animals and goods can introduce new host species and their associated parasites to new regions.

- Introducing invasive species like the Asian tiger mosquito (Aedes albopictus) to new regions has increased the risk of diseases like dengue and chikungunya in previously unaffected areas.

- The international livestock trade can introduce parasites not previously found in a region, impacting the local parasite landscape.

Human Activities and Infrastructure

Urban areas create microclimates and environmental conditions conducive to certain parasites and their vectors. Pollution and the presence of human-made water sources can provide breeding sites for disease vectors, causing adjustments to parasite distribution, such as:

- The proliferation of culex mosquitoes in urban environments contributed to the spread of the West Nile virus.
- The increased distribution of snail-borne diseases in areas with polluted water sources.

Veterinarians, public health officials, and ecologists need to monitor and adapt to these changes to prevent the spread of diseases and mitigate their impact on human and animal health. This may involve modifying vaccination protocols, implementing vector control measures, and enhancing surveillance and diagnostic capabilities to manage changing parasite landscapes effectively.

Emerging Parasitic Infections

Emerging parasitic diseases have either newly appeared or have significantly increased in incidence, geographic range, or host range. These diseases pose challenges for identification and management due to various factors.

Leishmaniasis

Leishmaniasis is caused by protozoan parasites of the leishmania genus and is transmitted through sandfly bites. This disease has shown signs of emergence in new regions, possibly due to climate change and human migration.

Leishmaniasis can manifest in various clinical forms, including cutaneous, visceral, and mucocutaneous. The diversity in its clinical presentation can make diagnosis challenging. Its symptoms may overlap with other diseases, leading to misdiagnosis and delayed treatment. Access to accurate diagnostic tools is limited in resource-limited regions, hindering timely diagnosis and treatment.

Chagas Disease

Chagas disease is caused by the parasite Trypanosoma cruzi and is primarily transmitted by triatomine bugs. It has extended beyond its traditional boundaries in Latin America. Chagas disease often remains asymptomatic for years, making early diagnosis difficult. Diagnostic tests for Chagas disease may have limited sensitivity and specificity, leading to false negatives. The triatomine bug is complex and requires sustained efforts to control the disease's vector.

Toxoplasmosis

Toxoplasmosis, caused by the parasite Toxoplasma gondii, has been recognized as an emerging disease in some regions. Many infections remain asymptomatic, making it challenging to identify and manage. T. gondii can infect many animals, making control and prevention complex. Routine screening for toxoplasmosis in pregnancy is not universally implemented, potentially missing cases in pregnant women.

Angiostrongyliasis

Angiostrongyliasis, caused by the parasitic nematode Angiostrongylus cantonensis, has also emerged in new regions. Lack of awareness: Many healthcare providers need to become more familiar with the disease. A lack of experience with it results in misdiagnosis or delayed diagnosis. Clinical manifestations can range from mild headache and nausea to severe neurological complications, making diagnosis challenging. There are no specific antiparasitic drugs for angiostrongyliasis, and management is primarily supportive.

Babesiosis

Babesiosis is caused by intraerythrocytic parasites of the babesia genus and is transmitted through tick bites. Cases have been emerging in new regions. Babesiosis mimics malaria symptoms, leading to misdiagnosis. The disease can range from mild flu-like symptoms to severe, life-threatening conditions, making it difficult to predict disease outcomes. Some babesia species have zoonotic potential, complicating the understanding of disease dynamics.

Dirofilariasis

Dirofilariasis is caused by filarial nematodes, particularly Dirofilaria immitis, and is transmitted by mosquitoes. The disease has expanded into new regions. Many infected individuals remain asymptomatic; the disease may only be discovered incidentally.

Altered climate conditions have expanded the habitat range of the disease vectors, increasing the risk of transmission to humans and pets. Dirofilariasis can be misdiagnosed as other respiratory conditions due to its diverse clinical manifestations.

Challenges in Identifying and Managing Emerging Parasitic Diseases

- **Diagnostic Limitations**: Many emerging parasitic diseases present with diverse or nonspecific symptoms, and diagnostic tools may lack sensitivity and specificity.

- **Globalization and Travel**: Increased travel and global trade facilitate the movement of parasites and disease vectors across borders.

- **Vector-Borne Diseases**: Controlling parasites transmitted by vectors (e.g., mosquitoes, ticks) can be challenging, especially when the vectors adapt to new environments.

- **Environmental Changes**: Alterations in ecosystems, including climate change, can impact parasite distribution and transmission dynamics.

- **Drug Resistance**: The emergence of drug-resistant strains can limit treatment options and increase the difficulty of disease management.

- **Zoonotic Transmission**: Many emerging parasitic diseases are zoonotic, creating complex epidemiological patterns and disease control challenges.

- **Limited Awareness**: Healthcare providers, public health systems, and communities may lack awareness of these emerging diseases, leading to delayed recognition and response.

Addressing these challenges requires a multifaceted approach, including improved surveillance, research, diagnostic tools, and public health education. It is crucial to remain vigilant and adapt to these emerging parasitic diseases to prevent their further spread and mitigate their impact on human and animal health.

Eco-Friendly Strategies

Adapting to climate-driven changes in parasite dynamics is paramount for sustaining livestock health and ensuring the resilience of agricultural systems. As climate change alters temperature and precipitation patterns, parasites that affect livestock are shifting in distribution, intensity, and seasonality. A range of strategies can be employed to address these challenges, each designed to mitigate the risks associated with evolving parasite dynamics. These strategies encompass monitoring and surveillance, breeding and genetics, pasture and grazing management, deworming practices, biosecurity, nutrition, parasite-resistant forages, and more. This comprehensive overview explores each of these strategies in detail.

Improved Monitoring and Surveillance

- **Regular Assessment:** Consistent monitoring and surveillance programs are pivotal. Regularly collect samples and data to assess the prevalence and intensity of parasitic infections in livestock populations.

- **Advanced Diagnostic Tools:** Use advanced diagnostic techniques like PCR-based tests and serological assays. These tools offer increased sensitivity and specificity in detecting parasitic infections, enabling more accurate and early diagnosis.

Climate-Resilient Breeding

- **Selective Breeding:** Select livestock breeds that exhibit resilience to climate-related stressors and parasitic infections. Breeding for resilience improves the overall health and productivity of livestock.

- **Resistance Traits:** Include resistance traits in your breeding objectives. These traits can reduce the reliance on chemical treatments and the associated risks of drug resistance.

Grazing Management

- **Rotational Grazing:** Implement rotational grazing practices to optimize pasture health and minimize parasite contamination. Regularly moving livestock to new pastures can break the parasite life cycle.

- **Adapted Schedules:** Adjust grazing schedules and stocking rates based on climate-driven changes in forage availability and parasite risk. This adaptive approach reduces the risk of overgrazing and pasture degradation.

Strategic Deworming

- **Informed Decision-Making:** Develop deworming strategies based on the data you've collected from monitoring your programs and environmental conditions. Avoid routine deworming and instead adopt targeted approaches.

- **Reduced Overuse:** Reducing unnecessary deworming helps mitigate the risk of developing drug resistance in parasite populations. Deworm only when indicated by monitoring results.

Biosecurity Measures

- **Preventing Introduction:** Establish strict biosecurity measures to prevent the introduction of new parasite strains or species through animal movements. Effective biosecurity includes quarantine protocols for incoming animals.

- **Isolation and Quarantine:** Isolate and quarantine newly introduced animals to prevent the spread of parasites. This practice minimizes the risk of disease transmission within the herd.

Nutritional Management

- **Dietary Adaptations:** Adjust livestock diets to address climate-induced nutritional deficiencies and support the immune system. Balanced nutrition helps animals cope with the stressors associated with parasitic infections.

- **Supplementary Nutrition:** To maintain livestock health and resilience, provide supplementary nutrition during periods of reduced forage availability, such as during droughts.

- **Forage Selection:** Select and plant forage varieties that resist certain parasites naturally. These forages may contain compounds that reduce the incidence of parasitic infections in livestock.

Alternative Treatments and Preventatives

- **Exploring Alternatives:** Explore alternative treatments and preventatives such as herbal remedies or biological control agents. These options can complement or replace traditional chemical treatments.

- **Parasitic Vaccines:** Consider using parasitic vaccines where they are available and appropriate for the specific parasites affecting livestock.

- **Anti-Parasitic Plants:** Certain plant species contain secondary compounds with anti-parasitic properties. For example, some tannin-rich forage plants can inhibit parasite development in the gut.
- **Parasite Control:** Encouraging livestock to consume these anti-parasitic plants can reduce parasite exposure and lessen the need for chemical treatments.

Integrated Pest Management (IPM)

- **Holistic Approach:** Implement an integrated pest management (IPM) approach that combines various strategies, including biological control methods (e.g., nematophagous fungi), targeted chemical treatments, and rotational grazing.
- **Environmental Considerations:** Prioritize IPM practices that minimize environmental impacts and preserve beneficial organisms while controlling parasite populations.

Research and Innovation

- **Scientific Investigation:** Invest in research to understand the specific impacts of climate change on local parasite dynamics. Research can inform adaptation strategies and improve their effectiveness.
- **Innovative Solutions:** Promote innovative solutions like developing climate-resistant livestock breeds and novel treatment methods that account for changing environmental conditions.

Collaboration and Knowledge Sharing

- **Stakeholder Collaboration:** Collaborate with local agricultural extension services, universities, and research institutions to access the latest information on parasite management in a changing climate.
- **Peer Exchange:** Share knowledge and experiences with other livestock producers and researchers to benefit from collective wisdom and best practices in parasite management.

Climate-Resilient Infrastructure

- **Livestock Housing:** Adapt livestock housing and infrastructure to cope with extreme weather events and temperature fluctuations. Ensure that animals have access to shade and proper ventilation during heatwaves and other climate-related stressors.

Diversification of Livestock Species

- **Species Variation:** Consider diversifying livestock species to adapt to changing conditions. Some species may be more resilient to certain parasites or better suited to altered environmental conditions, reducing the risk associated with monospecific farming.

- **Awareness:** Develop awareness of sustainable and climate-resilient practices while advocating for their adoption among stakeholders and the wider agricultural community.

Heat Stress Mitigation

Rising temperatures due to climate change can subject livestock to heat stress, which weakens their immune system, making them more susceptible to parasitic infections. To mitigate heat stress, ensure livestock can access shade, such as natural tree cover or purpose-built shelters. Adequate ventilation is crucial to prevent overheating. Nonetheless, providing access to cool, clean water sources helps maintain hydration and regulate body temperature.

Genetic Resistance

- **Breeding for Resistance:** Genetic resistance is selectively breeding livestock for inherent immunity or resistance to specific parasites.

- **Selective Breeding Programs:** Breeding programs can be established to develop livestock with natural resistance traits. For example, selecting animals with higher red blood cell counts may reduce susceptibility to blood-feeding parasites like haemonchus contortus.

- **Sustainable Parasite Control:** Genetic resistance can complement other parasite control strategies and reduce the reliance on chemical treatments.

Soil Improvement

- **Soil-Forage-Parasite Connection:** The health of the soil directly influences forage quality and quantity, which, in turn, affects livestock grazing patterns and susceptibility to parasitic infections.

- **Reseeding and Soil Amendments:** Practices like reseeding pastures with high-nutrient forages and soil amendments can improve soil health and forage quality. Healthy soils promote the growth of nutritious forage that supports livestock health and resilience.
- **Reduction in Parasite Exposure:** High-quality forage helps reduce the risk of parasitic infections by providing essential nutrients and supporting the well-being of livestock.

Remote Sensing and GIS

- **Environmental Data:** Remote sensing technologies, including satellite imagery and drones, can provide detailed environmental data.
- **Geospatial Analysis:** Geographic Information Systems (GIS) are used to integrate climate data, soil quality, and vegetation cover. Such analysis can predict disease risk and help you to plan grazing strategies based on climate data.

Integrating climate and environmental data into livestock management decisions allows for informed, data-driven approaches that reduce the risk of parasitic infections.

Seasonal Management

- **Adaptation to Climate Shifts:** Climate change causes seasonal shifts, impacting forage availability and parasite dynamics.
- **Breeding and Weaning:** Adapt livestock breeding and weaning schedules to align with climate-driven changes. This can help optimize the health and well-being of animals based on the timing of forage availability and parasite risk.

Flexibility in management practices is crucial to adapt to changing seasonal patterns and the associated challenges.

Climate-Resilient Livestock Shelters

- **Extreme Weather Protection:** Climate-resilient livestock shelters are designed to protect animals from extreme weather events, such as hurricanes, heavy rainfall, and extreme temperatures.
- **Stress Reduction:** Adequate shelter can reduce the stress experienced by livestock during adverse weather conditions. Stress reduction supports the immune system and decreases susceptibility to parasitic infections.

Shelter design should consider local climate conditions and the specific needs of the livestock species to be housed.

These comprehensive adaptation strategies address the multifaceted challenges climate-driven changes in parasite dynamics pose. Combined, they can contribute to the long-term health and sustainability of livestock systems in a changing climate. Collaboration among stakeholders and ongoing research is vital for tailoring these strategies to specific regions and ensuring their effectiveness.

Glossary of Terms and Parasite Reference

A – Z Glossary

- **Acquired Immunity –** Acquired immunity refers to the immune system's ability to recognize and remember specific pathogens, like parasites, after an initial exposure. This recognition allows the immune system to respond more effectively at subsequent encounters with the same pathogen.

- **Adaptation –** In the context of natural parasitic control, adaptation refers to the evolutionary process through which parasites and their hosts develop specific traits and behaviors that help them survive and reproduce in their respective environments. Parasites may adapt to exploit host resources or evade the host's immune system, while hosts may develop adaptive responses to resist parasitic infection. This ongoing adaptation process often leads to coevolution between parasites and their hosts.

- **Antagonistic Coevolution –** Antagonistic coevolution is a dynamic evolutionary relationship between parasites and their hosts in which each exerts selective pressure on the other. Parasites evolve strategies to exploit hosts, while hosts evolve defenses to resist or tolerate parasite infection. This constant back-and-forth competition drives the development of new traits and countermeasures in both parasites and hosts, resulting in an evolutionary arms race.

- **Antiparasitic Compounds** – Antiparasitic compounds are substances, often chemical or biological, used to target and eliminate parasitic infections. These compounds can include medications, such as antiparasitic drugs or herbal remedies, designed to kill or inhibit the growth of parasites. They are crucial for the treatment and control of parasitic diseases in both humans and animals.

- **Antiparasitic Drugs** – Antiparasitic drugs are pharmaceutical substances specifically formulated to treat parasitic infections in humans and animals. These drugs may target various types of parasites, including protozoa, helminths (worms), and ectoparasites like ticks and fleas. They work by disrupting the parasites' life cycles, metabolism, or reproductive processes, ultimately leading to their elimination from the host's body.

- **Behavioral Fever** – Behavioral fever is a phenomenon observed in some host species as a response to parasitic infection. When infected by certain parasites, hosts may exhibit an increase in body temperature as a deliberate behavioral response to combat the infection. This elevated temperature can create an environment less conducive to the parasite's survival and reproduction, contributing to the host's defense mechanisms.

- **Biological Control** – Biological control is a method of pest management that involves using natural enemies, like parasitoid wasps, predators, or pathogens, to regulate populations of pest species. In the context of natural parasitic control, biological control refers to using one parasite or organism to control another, often to reduce the impact of harmful parasites on ecosystems or agriculture.

- **Coevolution** – Coevolution is the simultaneous and reciprocal evolution of two or more species that interact closely with each other, like parasites and their hosts. In this process, each species exerts selective pressure on the other, developing characteristics and adaptations that allow them to exploit or defend against one another.

- **Commensalism** – Commensalism is a kind of symbiotic interaction in which the relationship between two species benefits one of the species while causing little to no harm or advantage to the other. When discussing interactions that result in one organism residing in a host without harming or benefiting from it in a way that lowers the population of harmful parasites, the term "commensalism" may be used concerning natural parasitic control.

- **Ectoparasite** – An ectoparasite is a type of parasite that lives on the external surface of its host. These parasites feed on the host's blood, skin, or other bodily fluids. Examples of ectoparasites include ticks, fleas, lice, and certain mites.

- **Eco-Epidemiology** – Eco-epidemiology is a field of study that examines the ecological and epidemiological factors influencing the transmission and spread of infectious diseases, including those caused by parasites.

- **Endoparasite** – An endoparasite is a parasite that lives inside the body of its host. These parasites can inhabit various internal organs or tissues and feed on the host's blood, tissues, or bodily fluids. Examples of endoparasites include tapeworms, liver flukes, and some protozoan parasites.

- **Entomopathogenic Fungi** – Entomopathogenic fungi are a group of fungi that are pathogenic to insects. They infect and kill a number of insect species and are often used as biological control agents to manage insect pests.

- **Host** – In the context of parasitism, the host is the organism that harbors and provides resources for the parasite. Hosts can be plants, animals, or even microorganisms, and they may experience harm or negative effects due to the parasite's presence.

- **Hyperparasitism** – Hyperparasitism is a form of parasitism in which one parasite is parasitized by another. In this relationship, the primary parasite, which is already living in or on a host, becomes the host for a secondary parasite. This secondary parasite may target the primary parasite for resources or reproduction.

- **Immune Response** – The immune response is the collective set of physiological and biochemical mechanisms that organisms, including hosts, use to defend against foreign invaders, such as parasites. When a parasite infects a host, the host's immune system initiates a response to recognize, neutralize, and eliminate the parasite. The nature of the immune response varies depending on the type of parasite and the host species.

- **Immunoparasitology** – Immunoparasitology is a branch of parasitology that focuses on the study of host immune responses to parasitic infections. It investigates how hosts recognize and combat parasitic invaders, the development of immune memory, and the mechanisms underlying resistance or susceptibility to parasitic diseases.

- **Integrated Pest Management** – Integrated pest management (IPM) is an ecological pest and parasitic control approach. It involves using multiple strategies, including biological control, cultural practices, and chemical treatments, to manage pests and parasites in agriculture, horticulture, and forestry while minimizing the environmental impact.

- **Intermediate Host** – An intermediate host is a host species that a parasite uses to complete a stage in its life cycle but not the sexual phase. Parasites often require multiple hosts in their life cycle, with the intermediate host serving as a transitional stage for the parasite's development before reaching the definitive host for reproduction.

- **Microbiome** – The microbiome is the community of microorganisms, including bacteria, fungi, viruses, and other microbes, that inhabit the body of a host organism. These microorganisms can play a crucial role in host-parasite interactions by influencing the host's immune response and overall health. Understanding the microbiome is essential for studying natural parasitic control.

- **Mutualism** – Mutualism is a type of symbiotic relationship between two species in which both partners benefit from the association. In the context of parasitic control, mutualistic interactions can occur when one organism, such as a microbe, helps the host resist or tolerate parasitic infections, leading to a mutually beneficial outcome for both parties.

- **Parasite Manipulation** – Parasite manipulation is a phenomenon where parasites, through various mechanisms, alter the behavior or physiology of their host organisms to promote their own survival and reproduction. This can include changes in host behavior that benefit the parasite, such as increased predation risk, ultimately aiding the parasite in completing its life cycle.

- **Parasitism** – Parasitism is a type of symbiotic relationship in which one organism (the parasite) benefits at the expense of another organism (the host). Parasites derive resources from the host, potentially causing harm or reducing the host's fitness. Parasitism is a fundamental concept in the study of natural parasitic control.

- **Phoresy** – Phoresy is a type of commensalism in which one organism uses another organism as a means of transport to a new location. In the context of natural parasitic control, phoresy may involve parasites or organisms that attach themselves to a host and use it to disperse to new environments.

- **Predation** – This is a biological interaction in which one organism (the predator) captures, kills, and consumes another organism (the prey) for food. Predation can play a role in controlling the populations of organisms, including parasites, within ecosystems.

- **Predatory Nematodes** – These are microscopic roundworms that feed on other organisms, including harmful parasitic nematodes. They are used in biological control to manage parasitic nematodes that affect plants, animals, and humans. Predatory nematodes help reduce the population of harmful parasites by preying on them.

- **Reservoir Host** – A reservoir host is a host species that carries and maintains a parasite, often serving as a source of infection for other hosts, including humans. Reservoir hosts can be important in the epidemiology of parasitic diseases, as they play a role in the persistence and transmission of the parasite.

- **Symbiosis** – Symbiosis is a broad ecological term that refers to the interaction between two different species that live together in close proximity. In the context of parasitic control, symbiotic relationships can include mutualism, commensalism, and parasitism, depending on the effects and benefits of the species involved.

- **Transmission** – Transmission refers to the process of passing parasites from one host to another. This can occur through various means, such as direct contact, ingestion, or vector-mediated transmission. Understanding the mechanisms of transmission is essential for controlling parasitic infections.

- **Trophic Cascade** – A trophic cascade is an ecological phenomenon where changes in the abundance or behavior of one species in an ecosystem result in cascading effects on other species at different trophic levels. In the context of natural parasitic control, trophic cascades may affect the population dynamics of parasites, their hosts, and their interactions.

- **Vector** – A vector is an organism, often an arthropod such as a mosquito or tick, that can transmit parasites or pathogens from one host to another. Vectors play a critical role in transmitting various parasitic diseases, including malaria, Lyme disease, and others.

- **Zoonosis** – Zoonosis is a disease that can be transmitted from animals to humans. Many parasitic diseases have zoonotic potential, and understanding the dynamics of zoonotic parasites is crucial for both animal and human health.

Common Livestock Parasites (and How to Deal with Them)

- **Gastrointestinal Nematodes (Roundworms):** Implement regular deworming schedules using appropriate anthelmintic drugs and practice pasture management to reduce exposure to infective larvae.

- **Coccidia**: Improve sanitation in livestock housing, provide clean water sources, and consider using coccidiostats in feed or water to control coccidiosis.

- **Ticks**: Apply acaricides or use integrated pest management strategies, including rotating pastures, to manage tick infestations.

- **Fleas and Lice**: Use livestock-specific insecticides or dips for effective control and maintain clean and dry living conditions for animals.

- **Mites (e.g., Sarcoptes and Demodex):** Treat affected animals with acaricides and isolate or cull severely infested individuals to prevent the spread.

- **Flies (e.g., Stable Flies and Horn Flies):** Use fly control methods such as fly traps, insecticide ear tags, or larvicides in manure management.

- **Liver Flukes:** Prevent liver fluke infection by managing water sources, controlling snail populations, and deworming livestock as necessary.

- **Lungworms:** Administer anthelmintic drugs targeting lungworms and practice good pasture management to reduce exposure.

- **Maggots (Myiasis):** Maintain good hygiene, clean wounds, and use fly repellents to prevent myiasis infestations.

- **Biting Midges (Culicoides):** Protect livestock from biting midges by using insect repellents and implementing measures to minimize breeding sites, such as standing water.

- **Babesia and Anaplasma (Tick-Borne Pathogens):** Control tick populations to reduce the risk of these bloodborne diseases and consider vaccination for some cases.

- **Scabies (Sarcoptic Mange):** Isolate and treat affected animals, as well as implement quarantine and treatment protocols to prevent the spread of scabies.

- **Foot Rot:** Isolate affected animals, maintain clean and dry environments, and use appropriate foot baths with disinfectants to manage foot rot.

- **Liver Abscesses:** Monitor and manage livestock nutrition, particularly in feedlot situations, to reduce the risk of liver abscesses.

- **Sheep Keds (Louse Flies):** Use insecticidal sprays, dips, or systemic insecticides to control sheep keds and ensure proper animal handling to minimize stress.

- **Cryptosporidium:** Improve sanitation, isolate infected animals, and provide supportive care to minimize the effects of cryptosporidiosis.

- **White Muscle Disease (Selenium and Vitamin E Deficiency):** Supplement livestock diets with selenium and vitamin E or provide free-choice mineral mixes to prevent this nutritional deficiency.

- **Bovine Tuberculosis**: Implement surveillance and testing programs, isolate and cull infected animals, and practice biosecurity measures to control bovine tuberculosis.

- **Tapeworms**: Deworm livestock with products effective against tapeworms and use good pasture management to reduce tapeworm exposure.

- **Tsetse Flies (African Trypanosomiasis)**: Use insecticide-treated targets or traps to control tsetse fly populations and implement tsetse fly control programs in affected regions.

- **Ectoparasitic Mites in Chickens (e.g., Northern Fowl Mites)**: Isolate and treat affected birds, clean and disinfect housing, and use acaricides to control mite infestations.

- **Lambing/Kidding Sickness**: Provide appropriate nutrition to pregnant ewes and does, monitor for pregnancy toxemia, and provide supportive care during lambing or kidding.

Conclusion

One of the most critical takeaways of this book is the mantra of "Rotation, rotation, rotation." Implementing a regular rotation schedule for your livestock, moving them into new pastures and paddocks at least every 60 days, is the cornerstone of a successful parasite management strategy. Consider shortening the rotation period to every 30 days for even better results, and during outbreaks or high-load times, increasing the frequency becomes the best practice. The power of effective pasture management through rotation cannot be overstated, as it minimizes exposure to parasites and encourages healthier living conditions for your animals.

Beyond rotation, maintaining clean and debris-free stable, coop, or cage areas is equally important. Regular cleaning, especially after deworming times, is essential to prevent reinfection. Utilizing drying agents like lime and diatomaceous earth can further improve your efforts in creating an environment less favorable for parasites.

An often overlooked aspect of parasite control is the health of pastures and water systems. Keeping water sources clean and ensuring your livestock refrain from drinking from ponds, creeks, puddles, or other potentially contaminated water sources is key. During extremely wet conditions, exercise caution and avoid grazing livestock on pastures with widespread manure and short forage.

Another vital strategy is putting a structured approach to deworming in place. Administer antiparasitics for at least three consecutive days every month with housed animals. Follow this with a free-choice lick containing fresh ingredients or herbs, or run your livestock through a beneficial plant paddock for three additional days. By creating bulk mixes and boluses and procuring the most ingredients online, you can streamline deworming practices, making them more efficient and cost-effective.

Recognize that some animals are more susceptible to parasitic infestations than others. They may show signs of reduced vitality or sluggishness compared to other animals within the group. These individuals should be monitored closely, with regular fecal samples collected and analyzed. Consider culling these animals if feasible, especially if their susceptibility is due to poor eating habits or a lack of consumption of antiparasitic forages. Preventing the passage of these poor habits to their offspring is crucial for improving your herd or flock overall.

With these strategies in place, the need for frequent fecal tests will diminish, and the battle against internal parasites will no longer be a time-consuming chore. Your livestock will thrive in a healthier, more sustainable environment, and you'll have the peace of mind that comes with knowing that you've mastered the power of natural parasite management.

By embracing the practices outlined in this book and tailoring them to your specific circumstances and animals, you'll unlock the potential for a healthy, resilient herd or flock. With ongoing dedication to these strategies, you'll protect your livestock and build a future where the relentless pursuit of parasite management transforms into a harmonious and part-time aspect of your livestock care routine.

The well-being of your animals and the success of your livestock operation are within your reach. The journey may have started with questions and concerns, but now it ends with knowledge, empowerment, and a brighter future for your livestock and land.

Here's another book by Dion Rosser that you might like

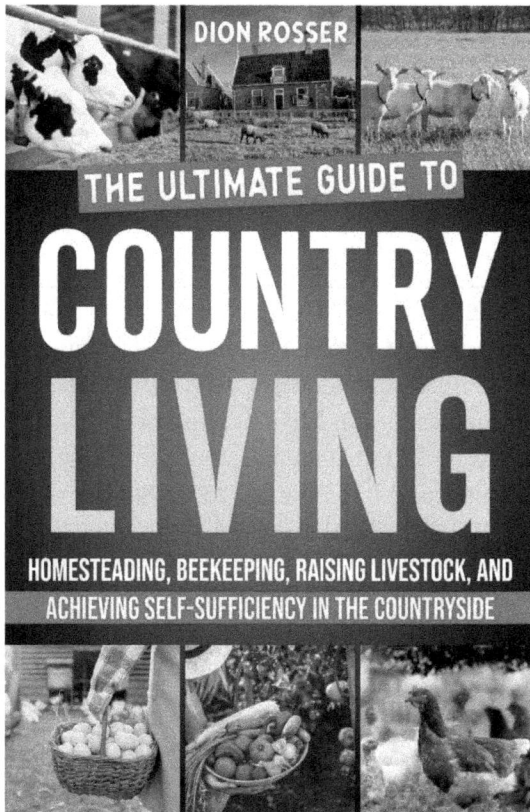

DION ROSSER

THE ULTIMATE GUIDE TO

COUNTRY LIVING

HOMESTEADING, BEEKEEPING, RAISING LIVESTOCK, AND
ACHIEVING SELF-SUFFICIENCY IN THE COUNTRYSIDE

References

(N.d.-a). Nih.gov. https://www.ncbi.nlm.nih.gov/pmc/articles/PMC7767362/

(N.d.-b). Nih.gov.
https://www.ncbi.nlm.nih.gov/pmc/articles/PMC5756309/#:~:text=Background
%3A,activities%20including%20anti%2Dparasitic%20effect.

A brief history of parasitology. (2023, March 3). Veterinary Practice.
https://www.veterinary-practice.com/article/history-of-parasitology

A guide to herbal remedies. (n.d.). Medlineplus.gov.
https://medlineplus.gov/ency/patientinstructions/000868.htm

Ahmed, M., M.D. Laing, and I.V. Nsahlai. 2013. Studies on the ability of two
isolates of Bacillus thuringiensis, an isolate of Clonostachys rosea f. rosea, and a
diatomaceous earth product, to control gastrointestinal nematodes of sheep.
Biocontrol Science and Technology.

Alok, A. (2015). Curcumin – pharmacological actions and its role in oral
submucous fibrosis: A review. Journal of Clinical and Diagnostic Research:
JCDR, 9(10), ZE01. https://doi.org/10.7860/jcdr/2015/13857.6552

Alzohairy, M. A. (2016). Therapeutics role of Azadirachta indica (neem) and
their active constituents in disease prevention and treatment. Evidence-Based
Complementary and Alternative Medicine: eCAM, 2016, 1–11.
https://doi.org/10.1155/2016/7382506

Amalraj, A., Pius, A., Gopi, S., & Gopi, S. (2017). Biological activities of
curcuminoids, other biomolecules from turmeric and their derivatives – A
review. Journal of Traditional and Complementary Medicine, 7(2), 205–233.
https://doi.org/10.1016/j.jtcme.2016.05.005

Animal husbandry – Nature Neem. (n.d.). Natureneem.com.
https://natureneem.com/en/solutions/animal-husbandry

Anthelmintic. (n.d.). Herbal Reality. https://www.herbalreality.com/western-action/anthelmintic/

Athanasiadou, S., Githiori, J., & Kyriazakis, I. (2007). Medicinal plants for helminth parasite control: facts and fiction. Animal: An International Journal of Animal Bioscience, 1(9), 1392–1400. https://doi.org/10.1017/s1751731107000730

Aylott, R. I. (2003). GIN | The Product and its Manufacture. In Encyclopedia of Food Sciences and Nutrition (pp. 2889–2893). Elsevier.

Azarpajouh, S. (2022, November 15). Breeding for parasite resistance in dairy cows. Dairy Global. https://www.dairyglobal.net/health-and-nutrition/health/breeding-for-parasite-resistance-in-dairy-cows/

Bang KS, Familton AS, Sykes AR (1990) Effect of copper oxide wire particle treatment on establishment of major gastrointestinal nematodes in lambs. Research in Veterinary Science 49:132-139

Barkley, M. (n.d.). Prevent parasites through grazing management. Psu.edu. https://extension.psu.edu/prevent-parasites-through-grazing-management

Beltran, M. A. G., & Martin, R. J. (2015, September 1). Home page. Doi.Org; unknown. https://doi.org/

Best management practices for pasture parasite management. (2019, May 6). Cornell University College of Veterinary Medicine. https://www.vet.cornell.edu/animal-health-diagnostic-center/programs/nyschap/modules-documents/best-management-practices-pasture-parasite-management

Better for animals. (n.d.). Soilassociation.org. https://www.soilassociation.org/take-action/organic-living/why-organic/better-for-animals/

Biosecurity, L. (n.d.-a). Histopathology sampling guide for livestock. Gov.au. https://www.agric.wa.gov.au/livestock-biosecurity/histopathology-sampling-guide-livestock

Biosecurity, L. (n.d.-b). Livestock disease veterinary sampling guide. Gov.au. https://www.agric.wa.gov.au/livestock-biosecurity/livestock-disease-veterinary-sampling-guide

Bissa, S., & Bohra, A. (2011). Antibacterial potential of pot marigold. Academicjournals.org. https://academicjournals.org/journal/JMA/article-full-text-pdf/F3AA1F49795

Bom Harris, D. V. M. (2020, September 1). Prevent parasites with pasture management. Old-Dominion-Vets. https://www.olddominionvets.com/post/prevent-parasites-with-pasture-management

Bosco, A., Prigioniero, A., Falzarano, A., Maurelli, M. P., Rinaldi, L., Cringoli, G., Quaranta, G., Claps, S., Sciarrillo, R., Guarino, C., & Scarano, P. (2023). Use of perennial plants in the fight against gastrointestinal nematodes of sheep. Frontiers in Parasitology, 2, 1186149. https://doi.org/10.3389/fpara.2023.1186149

Brief history herbal Medicine. (2018, May 16). Herbal Clinic – Swansea. https://www.herbalclinic-swansea.co.uk/herbal-medicine/a-brief-history-of-herbal-medicine/

Burke JM, Miller JE, Olcott DD, Olcott BM, Terrill TH (2004) Effect of copper oxide wire particles dosage and feed supplement level on Haemonchus contortus infection in lambs Veterinary Parasitology 123:235– 243

Cattle tick fever. (n.d.). MLA Corporate. https://www.mla.com.au/research-and-development/animal-health-welfare-and-biosecurity/parasites/identification/cattle-tick-fever/

Climate change and the expansion of animal and zoonotic diseases – what is the agency's contribution? (2021, June 2). Iaea.org. https://www.iaea.org/resources/news-article/climate-change-and-the-expansion-of-animal-and-zoonotic-diseases-what-is-the-agencys-contribution

Climate impacts on agriculture and food supply. (n.d.). Chicago.gov. https://climatechange.chicago.gov/climate-impacts/climate-impacts-agriculture-and-food-supply

Coates, J. (2012, October 25). The history and use of herbal medicine and its use today for pets. Petmd.com; PetMD. https://www.petmd.com/blogs/fullyvetted/2012/oct/history_and_use_of_herbal_medicine_and_use_in_pets-29279

coccidiosis. (n.d.). MLA Corporate. https://www.mla.com.au/research-and-development/animal-health-welfare-and-biosecurity/parasites/identification/coccidiosis/

Common cattle parasites. (2023, September 18). Texas A&M AgriLife Extension Service. https://agrilifeextension.tamu.edu/asset-external/common-cattle-parasites/

Common internal parasites of cattle. (n.d.). Missouri.edu. https://extension.missouri.edu/publications/g2130

D., l. L. H. (n.d.). Economic impact of gastrointestinal parasitism in Amazon buffalo far- Brazil. Embrapa.Br. https://www.alice.cnptia.embrapa.br/alice/bitstream/doc/403427/1/Economicimpact.pdf

Dai, Y.-L., Li, Y., Wang, Q., Niu, F.-J., Li, K.-W., Wang, Y.-Y., Wang, J., Zhou, C.-Z., & Gao, L.-N. (2022). Chamomile: A review of its traditional uses, chemical constituents, pharmacological activities and quality control studies.

Molecules (Basel, Switzerland), 28(1), 133.
https://doi.org/10.3390/molecules28010133

DIATOMACEOUS EARTH as an alternative treatment for internal parasites.
(n.d.). SA Mohair Growers. https://www.angoras.co.za/article/diatomaceous-earth-as-an-alternative-treatment-for-internal-parasites

Diatomaceous Earth. (n.d.). Mdsmallruminant.
https://www.sheepandgoat.com/de

Dotto, J. M., & Chacha, J. S. (2020). The potential of pumpkin seeds as a functional food ingredient: A review. Scientific African, 10(e00575), e00575.
https://doi.org/10.1016/j.sciaf.2020.e00575

Eminov: Effect of certain pasture plants on gastrointesti... – Google Scholar.
(n.d.). Google.Com.
https://scholar.google.com/scholar_lookup?journal=Sov+Agric+Sci&title=Effect+of+certain+pasture+plants+on+gastrointestinal+nematodes+of+sheep&author=RS+Eminov&volume=1&publication_year=1982&pages=72-74&

ESCCAP. (n.d.). Glossary. Esccap.org. https://www.esccap.org/glossary/

Faculty By Department, & Find a Physician. (n.d.). Aloe. Rochester.edu.
https://www.urmc.rochester.edu/encyclopedia/content.aspx?contenttypeid=19&contentid=Aloe

Farmacy. (2023, May 2). Managing your pasture to master the parasites.
Farmacy. https://www.farmacy.co.uk/article/415-managing-your-pasture-to-master-the-parasites

Farmers Guardian. (2021, July 8). Management of pasture for parasite control.
Farmersguardian.com.
https://www.farmersguardian.com/sponsored/4092600/management-pasture-parasite-control

Ferguson, D., & Vogt, W. (2019, May 15). Fact sheet: Poisonous plants for cattle. Beefmagazine.com

flies. (n.d.). MLA Corporate. https://www.mla.com.au/research-and-development/animal-health-welfare-and-biosecurity/parasites/identification/flies/

Gastrointestinal worms. (n.d.). MLA Corporate.
https://www.mla.com.au/research-and-development/animal-health-welfare-and-biosecurity/parasites/identification/gastrointestinal-worms/

Getting rid of intestinal parasites with diatomaceous earth. (n.d.).
Www.Sassyorganics.Com.Au. https://www.sassyorganics.com.au
https://www.sassyorganics.com.au/blog/our-blog/getting-rid-of-intestinal-parasites-with-diatomace/

Glossary. (n.d.-a). Cornell.edu.
https://biocontrol.entomology.cornell.edu/glossary.php

Glossary. (n.d.-b). Ucanr.edu. https://ipm.ucanr.edu/PMG/glossary.html

Gupta. (2010). Chamomile: A herbal medicine of the past with a bright future (Review). Molecular Medicine Reports, 3(6), 895. https://doi.org/10.3892/mmr.2010.377

Hajaji, S., Alimi, D., Jabri, M. A., Abuseir, S., Gharbi, M., & Akkari, H. (2018). Anthelmintic activity of Tunisian chamomile (Matricaria recutita L.) against Haemonchus contortus. Journal of Helminthology, 92(2), 168–177. https://doi.org/10.1017/s0022149x17000396

Herbal medicine. (2021, September 24). Hopkinsmedicine.org. https://www.hopkinsmedicine.org/health/wellness-and-prevention/herbal-medicine

Herbal worming for cattle – McDowell's herbal treatments. (n.d.). McDowell's Herbal Treatments. https://www.mcdowellsherbal.com/success-stories-for-dogs/50-treatments/bovine-treatments/644-herbal-worming-for-cattle

Homemade herbal animal dewormer & tonic. (n.d.). Libertyhomesteadfarm.com. https://libertyhomesteadfarm.com/herbal-remedies/homemade-herbal-animal-dewormer-tonic/

How to work with your vet for the best farm outcomes. (2023, February 16). Pasture.Io. https://pasture.io/farm-animal-health/working-with-your-vet

Islam, M. S., & Rahman, M. M. (2016). Diatomaceous earth-induced alterations in the reproductive attributes in the housefly Musca domestica L. (Diptera: Muscidae). SSRN Electronic Journal, 96, 41241–41244. https://doi.org/10.2139/ssrn.3856328

Jaja, I., & Ungeviwa, P. (2022). A 6-year retrospective report of livestock parasitic diseases in the Eastern Cape Province, South Africa. Open Veterinary Journal, 12(2), 204. https://doi.org/10.5455/ovj.2022.v12.i2.8

Klasing, K. C., & Leshchinsky, T. V. (2000). Interactions between nutrition and immunity: Lessons from animal agriculture. In Nutrition and Immunology (pp. 363–373). Humana Press.

Kumar, N., Rao, T. K. S., Varghese, A., & Rathor, V. S. (2013). Internal parasite management in grazing livestock. Journal of Parasitic Diseases: Official Organ of the Indian Society for Parasitology, 37(2), 151–157. https://doi.org/10.1007/s12639-012-0215-z

Lefrançois, T., & Pineau, T. (2014). Public health and livestock: Emerging diseases in food animals. Animal Frontiers, 4(1), 4–6. https://doi.org/10.2527/af.2014-0001

Lice. (n.d.). MLA Corporate. https://www.mla.com.au/research-and-development/animal-health-welfare-and-biosecurity/parasites/identification/lice/

Liver fluke. (n.d.). MLA Corporate. https://www.mla.com.au/research-and-development/animal-health-welfare-and-biosecurity/parasites/identification/liver-fluke/

Livestock and poultry infectious diseases: Pathogenesis and immune mechanisms. (n.d.). Frontiersin.org. https://www.frontiersin.org/research-topics/47450/livestock-and-poultry-infectious-diseases-pathogenesis-and-immune-mechanisms

Livestock disease: Cause and control – Oklahoma state university. (2017, March 1). Okstate.edu. https://extension.okstate.edu/fact-sheets/livestock-disease-cause-and-control.html

Livestock management. (2018, August 28). Rodale Institute. https://rodaleinstitute.org/why-organic/organic-farming-practices/livestock-management/

Livestock parasites. (n.d.). Gov.au. https://www.agric.wa.gov.au/livestock-animals/livestock-management/livestock-parasites

M. WIEWIÓRA , M. ŁUKASIEWICZ , J. BARTOSIK , M. MAKARSKI, T. NIEMIEC. (2015). Diatomaceous earth in the prevention of worm infestation in purebred pigeons. Ann. Warsaw Univ. of Life Sci. – SGGW Animal Science, 54(2).

Mahleyuddin, N. N., Moshawih, S., Ming, L. C., Zulkifly, H. H., Kifli, N., Loy, M. J., Sarker, M. M. R., Al-Worafi, Y. M., Goh, B. H., Thuraisingam, S., & Goh, H. P. (2021). Coriandrum sativum L.: A review on ethnopharmacology, phytochemistry, and cardiovascular benefits. Molecules (Basel, Switzerland), 27(1), 209. https://doi.org/10.3390/molecules27010209

Mandal, S., & Mandal, M. (2015). Coriander (Coriandrum sativum L.) essential oil: Chemistry and biological activity. Asian Pacific Journal of Tropical Biomedicine, 5(6), 421–428. https://doi.org/10.1016/j.apjtb.2015.04.001

Mao, Q.-Q., Xu, X.-Y., Cao, S.-Y., Gan, R.-Y., Corke, H., Trust Beta, & Li, H.-B. (2019). Bioactive Compounds and Bioactivities of Ginger (Zingiber officinale Roscoe). Foods (Basel, Switzerland), 8(6), 185. https://doi.org/10.3390/foods8060185

Marcogliese, D. J. (2001). Implications of climate change for parasitism of animals in the aquatic environment. Canadian Journal of Zoology, 79(8), 1331–1352. https://doi.org/10.1139/z01-067

Marigold (Calendula). (2019, April 16). WholisticMatters. https://wholisticmatters.com/herb-detail/marigold-calendula/

Marosi, G., Szolnoki, B., Bocz, K., & Toldy, A. (2017). Fire-retardant recyclable and biobased polymer composites. In Novel Fire Retardant Polymers and Composite Materials (pp. 117–146). Elsevier.

Medicinal herb recipes for livestock. (n.d.). Sarahflackconsulting.com. https://www.sarahflackconsulting.com/articles/medicinal-herb-recipes-for-livestock/

Ndao, M. (2009). Diagnosis of parasitic diseases: Old and new approaches. Interdisciplinary Perspectives on Infectious Diseases, 2009, 1–15. https://doi.org/10.1155/2009/278246

Ntare, K. (n.d.). Natural herbs for treating Livestock. – Jaguza Farm Support. Jaguzafarm.com. https://jaguzafarm.com/support/natural-herbs-for-treating-livestock/

Nutrient management on livestock farms: Tips for feeding. (n.d.). Rutgers.edu. https://njaes.rutgers.edu/fs1064/

Parasites and Strategic Deworming. (n.d.). The College of Veterinary Medicine at Michigan State University. https://cvm.msu.edu/hospital/services/equine-services/for-owners/general-conditions-and-seeing-your-vet/parasites-and-strategic-deworming

Parasites, Diseases, and Control Measures. (n.d.). Usda.Gov. https://www.nal.usda.gov/exhibits/speccoll/exhibits/show/parasitic-diseases-with-econom/parasitic-diseases-with-econom

Parasites, diseases, and control measures. (n.d.). Usda.gov. https://www.nal.usda.gov/exhibits/speccoll/exhibits/show/parasitic-diseases-with-econom/parasitic-diseases-with-econom

Parasites, diseases, and control measures. (n.d.). Usda.gov. https://www.nal.usda.gov/exhibits/speccoll/exhibits/show/parasitic-diseases-with-econom/parasitic-diseases-with-econom

Parasites. (n.d.). MLA Corporate. https://www.mla.com.au/research-and-development/animal-health-welfare-and-biosecurity/parasites/

parasites. (n.d.). MLA Corporate. https://www.mla.com.au/research-and-development/animal-health-welfare-and-biosecurity/parasites/

Parasites. (n.d.). MLA Corporate. https://www.mla.com.au/research-and-development/animal-health-welfare-and-biosecurity/parasites/

Pasture management to control cattle worms. (2022, July 26). WormBoss. https://wormboss.com.au/management/non-chemical-worm-control-methods/pasture-management/

Pilarczyk, B., Tomza-Marciniak, A., Pilarczyk, R., Sadowska, N., Udała, J., & Kuba, J. (2022). The effect of season and meteorological conditions on parasite infection in farm-maintained mouflons (Ovis aries musimon). Journal of Parasitology Research, 2022, 1165782. https://doi.org/10.1155/2022/1165782

Plants poisonous to livestock. (n.d.). Missouri.edu. https://extension.missouri.edu/publications/g4970

Płoneczka-Janeczko, K., Szalińska, W., Otop, I., Piekarska, J., & Rypuła, K. (2023). Weather parameters as a predictive tool potentially allowing for better monitoring of dairy cattle against gastrointestinal parasites hazard. Scientific Reports, 13(1), 1–12. https://doi.org/10.1038/s41598-023-32890-0

Rahmani, A. H., Al shabrmi, F. M., & Aly, S. M. (2014). Active ingredients of ginger as potential candidates in the prevention and treatment of diseases via modulation of biological activities. International Journal of Physiology, Pathophysiology and Pharmacology, 6(2), 125.

Rahmann, G., & Seip, H. (n.d.). Bioactive forage and phytotherapy to cure and control endo-parasite diseases in sheep and goat farming systems – a review of current scientific knowledge. Orgprints.Org. https://orgprints.org/id/eprint/12976/1/181_Endoparasiten_Artikel_no_2_von_Rahmann_und_Seip.pdf

Richards, L. (2022, May 31). Wormwood: Uses, benefits, and risks. Medicalnewstoday.com. https://www.medicalnewstoday.com/articles/wormwood

Rizwan, H., Sajid, M., Shamim, A., Abbas, H., Qudoos, A., Maqbool, M., Malik, M., & Amin, Z. (2021). Sheep parasitism and its control by medicinal plants: A review. Parasitologists United Journal, 14(2), 112–121. https://doi.org/10.21608/puj.2021.70534.1114

Salehi, A., Razavi, M., & Vahedi Nouri, N. (2022). Seasonal prevalence of helminthic infections in the gastrointestinal tract of sheep in Mazandaran province, northern Iran. Journal of Parasitology Research, 2022, 7392801. https://doi.org/10.1155/2022/7392801

Sandoval-Castro, C. A., Torres-Acosta, J. F. J., Hoste, H., Salem, A. Z. M., & Chan-Pérez, J. I. (2012). Using plant bioactive materials to control gastrointestinal tract helminths in livestock. Animal Feed Science and Technology, 176(1–4), 192–201. https://doi.org/10.1016/j.anifeedsci.2012.07.023

Sego, S. (2015, October 1). Managing benign prostatic hypertrophy with pumpkin seeds. Clinical Advisor. https://www.clinicaladvisor.com/home/features/alternative-meds-update/managing-benign-prostatic-hypertrophy-with-pumpkin-seeds/

Shang, A., Cao, S.-Y., Xu, X.-Y., Gan, R.-Y., Tang, G.-Y., Corke, H., Mavumengwana, V., & Li, H.-B. (2019). Bioactive compounds and biological functions of garlic (Allium sativum L.). Foods (Basel, Switzerland), 8(7), 246. https://doi.org/10.3390/foods8070246

Signs of worms in cattle. (2022, July 25). WormBoss. https://wormboss.com.au/about-worms/signs-of-worms/

Smith, J. (2019, June 20). Managing parasites in livestock. EcoFarming Daily. https://www.ecofarmingdaily.com/raise-healthy-livestock/cattle/managing-parasites-livestock/

Species and Life Cycles. (n.d.). Org.Uk. https://www.scops.org.uk/internal-parasites/worms/species-and-lifecycles/

Straub, C. (2023, March 12). Simple herbal remedies for your homestead animals. Biome Munch. https://biome-munch.com/2023/03/12/simple-herbal-remedies-for-your-homestead-animals/

Surjushe, A., Vasani, R., & Saple, D. G. (2008). Aloe vera: A short review. Indian Journal of Dermatology, 53(4), 163. https://doi.org/10.4103/0019-5154.44785

Sustainable parasite control for sheep and goats. (n.d.). Msstate.edu. http://extension.msstate.edu/publications/sustainable-parasite-control-for-sheep-and-goats

Sykes, A. R. (1994). Parasitism and production in farm animals. Animal Science (Penicuik, Scotland), 59(2), 155–172. https://doi.org/10.1017/s0003356100007649

Tavares, L., Santos, L., & Zapata Noreña, C. P. (2021). Bioactive compounds of garlic: A comprehensive review of encapsulation technologies, characterization of the encapsulated garlic compounds and their industrial applicability. Trends in Food Science & Technology, 114, 232–244. https://doi.org/10.1016/j.tifs.2021.05.019

The history of herbal medicine. (n.d.). New Chapter. https://www.newchapter.com/wellness-blog/the-history-of-herbal-medicine/

Theileriosis. (n.d.). MLA Corporate. https://www.mla.com.au/research-and-development/animal-health-welfare-and-biosecurity/parasites/identification/theileriosis/

Ticks. (n.d.). MLA Corporate. https://www.mla.com.au/research-and-development/animal-health-welfare-and-biosecurity/parasites/identification/ticks/

Tipsheet: Organic management of internal and external livestock parasites. (n.d.). Ncat.org. https://attra.ncat.org/publication/tipsheet-organic-management-of-internal-and-external-livestock-parasites/

Top natural remedy tips for common ailments in cattle. (n.d.). Farmcompare.Com. https://www.farmcompare.com/news/top-natural-remedy-tips-for-common-ailments-in-cattle

Toppo, A. (2018, December 10). Important livestock management tips for farmers. Krishi Jagran Media Group. https://krishijagran.com/animal-husbandry/important-livestock-management-tips-for-farmers/

Toxoplasma gondii – Learn About Parasites – Western College of Veterinary Medicine. (n.d.). Learn About Parasites. https://wcvm.usask.ca/learnaboutparasites/parasites/toxoplasma-gondii-zoonoses.php

Trichomoniasis. (n.d.). MLA Corporate. https://www.mla.com.au/research-and-development/animal-health-welfare-and-biosecurity/diseases/reproductive/trichomoniasis/

Vinje, E. (2014, February 17). The history of herbs and herbal medicine. Planet Natural. https://www.planetnatural.com/herb-gardening-guru/history/

Vlasova, A. N., & Saif, L. J. (2021). Bovine immunology: Implications for dairy cattle. Frontiers in Immunology, 12. https://doi.org/10.3389/fimmu.2021.643206

Vogt, W. (2023, April 27). Are parasite problems returning in cattle due to dewormer resistance? Beefmagazine.com. https://www.beefmagazine.com/cattle-disease/are-parasite-problems-returning-in-cattle-due-to-dewormer-resistance-

Waller, P. J., Bernes, G., Thamsborg, S. M., Sukura, A., Richter, S. H., Ingebrigtsen, K., & Höglund, J. (2001). Plants as DE-worming agents of livestock in the Nordic countries: Historical perspective, popular beliefs and prospects for the future. Acta Veterinaria Scandinavica, 42(1), 31. https://doi.org/10.1186/1751-0147-42-31

Website, N. H. S. (2022, October 19). Herbal medicines. Nhs.uk. https://www.nhs.uk/conditions/herbal-medicines/

Willis. (2020, April 8). Benefits of natural products for animals — Natural Animal Health. Natural Animal Health. https://www.naturalanimalhealth.co.uk/blog/benefits-natural-products-animals

Windon, R. G. (1990). Selective breeding for the control of nematodiasis in sheep: -EN- -FR- -ES-. Revue Scientifique et Technique (International Office of Epizootics), 9(2), 555–576. https://doi.org/10.20506/rst.9.2.496

Wong, C. (2004, April 26). Do parasite cleanses really work? Verywell Health. https://www.verywellhealth.com/natural-remedies-for-intestinal-parasites-88232

Wormers and the soil. (2020, December 18). FAS; Farm Advisory Scotland. https://www.fas.scot/article/wormers-and-the-soil/